DATE DUE

Modern Critical Interpretations

William Shakespeare's
The Tempest

Modern Critical Interpretations

These and other titles in preparation

Modern Critical Interpretations

William Shakespeare's
The Tempest

Edited and with an introduction by

Harold Bloom
Sterling Professor of the Humanities
Yale University

Chelsea House Publishers ◊ *1988*
NEW YORK ◊ NEW HAVEN ◊ PHILADELPHIA

© 1988 by Chelsea House Publishers, a division
of Chelsea House Educational Communications, Inc.,
    345 Whitney Avenue, New Haven, CT 06511
    95 Madison Avenue, New York, NY 10016
    5068B West Chester Pike, Edgemont, PA 19028

Introduction © 1988 by Harold Bloom

Printed and bound in the United States of America

10 9 8 7 6 5 4 3 2 1

∞ The paper used in this publication meets the minimum
requirements of the American National Standard for
Permanence of Paper for Printed Library Materials,
Z39.48-1984.

Library of Congress Cataloging-in-Publication Data
William Shakespeare's The tempest.
    (Modern critical interpretations)
    Bibliography: p.
    Includes index.
    1. Shakespeare, William, 1564–1616. The tempest.
I. Bloom, Harold. II. Series.
PR2833.W48   1988   822.3'3   87-23902
ISBN 0-87754-940-0 (alk. paper)

Contents

Editor's Note

This book brings together a representative selection of the best modern critical interpretations of Shakespeare's romance *The Tempest*. The critical essays are reprinted here in the chronological order of their original publication. I am grateful to Dennis Fawcett and Susan Laity for their assistance in editing this volume.

My introduction, a defense of Caliban, finds Prospero therefore a somewhat problematic hero. Harry Berger, Jr., begins the chronological sequence of criticism with his remarkable exegesis of *The Tempest*, culminating in the question of whether Prospero truly desires to leave the island, or delays so as not to do so.

In a related reading, Marjorie Garber sees, as Berger does, the play struggling with definitions of the human and with human limitations, and invokes Renaissance glosses upon Daedalus to help illuminate Prospero. A brief New Historicist account of Caliban by Stephen J. Greenblatt complements Berger and Garber on the question of the limits of the human in *The Tempest* and so is inserted here, out of strict chronological order.

Julian Patrick's essay centers upon the play's concern with time, exploring its complex temporal organization. A comparison of the comic metastance of *The Tempest* with the tragic stance of *King Lear*, in James P. Driscoll's essay, is followed by Stephen Orgel's investigation of the female principle in *The Tempest*. Barbara Howard Traister analyzes Prospero's position as a magician within Renaissance dramatic tradition.

This book concludes with a New Historicist reading of *The Tempest* by Paul Brown. Little as I sympathize with attempts to relate Shakespeare to "the discourse of colonialism," I find exemplary Brown's emphasis upon the radical ambivalence of the play's conclusion.

Introduction

The Tempest is not a mystery play, offering a secret insight into human finalities; act 5 of *Hamlet* is closer to that. Perhaps *The Tempest* does turn ironically upon Shakespeare's conscious farewell to his dramatic art, but such an irony or allegory does not enhance the play's meanings. I sometimes think *The Tempest* was the first significant drama in which not much happens, beyond its protagonist's abandonment of his scheme of justified revenge precisely when he has all his enemies in his power. Most explanations of Prospero's refusal to take revenge reduce to the formulaic observation: "That's the way things turn out in Shakespeare's late romances." Let us move again towards the question: why does Prospero not gratify himself by fulfilling his revenge?

The originality of representation in *The Tempest* embraces only Prospero, the supernatural Ariel, compounded of fire and air, and the preternatural Caliban, compounded of earth and water. Unlike *The Winter's Tale*, *The Tempest* contrives to be a romance of the marvelous without ever being outrageous; the Shakespearean exuberance expresses itself here by cheerfully discarding any semblance of a plot.

Prospero, who is almost always sympathetic as Miranda's father, is dubiously fair to Ariel, and almost too grimly censorious towards the wretched Caliban. His peculiar severity towards Ferdinand also darkens him. But only this split, between loving father and puritanical hermeticist, makes Prospero truly interesting. He does not move our imagination as Ariel does, and Ariel, a kind of revised Puck, is less original a representation than Caliban is. Caliban does not run off with the play, as Barnardine does in *Measure for Measure,* but he makes us wonder how much humanity Prospero has sacrificed in exchange for hermetic knowledge and wisdom.

Caliban is uncanny to us, in precisely Freud's sense of "the uncanny." Something long estranged from us, yet still familiar, returns from repression in Caliban. We can be repelled by Caliban's degradation and by his de-

1

formity, but like Prospero we have to acknowledge that Caliban is somehow ours, not to be repudiated. It is not clear to me whether Caliban is meant to be wholly human, as there is something amphibian about him, and his mother Sycorax, like the weird sisters in *Macbeth*, has her preternatural aspects. What is certain is that Caliban has aesthetic dignity, and that the play is not wholly Prospero's only because of him. You could replace Ariel by various sprites (though not without loss), but you would not have *The Tempest* if you removed Caliban.

Why Shakespeare called the play *The Tempest* I cannot understand. Perhaps he should have called it *Prospero* or even *Prospero and Caliban*. Though the "names of the actors" describes Caliban as a "savage and deformed slave," I have never known any reader or theatergoer who could regard that as an adequate account of what may be Shakespeare's most deeply troubling single representation after Shylock. Robert Browning's Caliban, in the great monologue "Caliban upon Setebos," seems to me the most remarkable interpretation yet ventured, surpassing all overt literary criticism, and so I will employ it here as an aid, while yielding to all those who would caution me that Browning's Caliban is not Shakespeare's. Yes, but whose Caliban is?

Prospero forgives his enemies (and evidently will pardon Caliban) because he achieves a complex stance that hovers between the disinterestedness of the Hamlet of act 5, and a kind of hermetic detachment from his own powers, perhaps because he sees that even those are dominated by a temporal ebb and flow. But there is also a subtle sense in which Prospero has been deeply wounded by his failure to raise up a higher Caliban, even as Caliban is palpably hurt (in many senses) by Prospero. Their relations, throughout the play, are not less than dreadful and wound us also, as they seem to have wounded Browning, judging by his Caliban's meditation:

> Himself peeped late, eyed Prosper at his books
> Careless and lofty, lord now of the isle:
> Vexed, 'stiched a book of broad leaves, arrow-shaped,
> Wrote thereon, he knows what, prodigious words;
> Has peeled a wand and called it by a name;
> Weareth at whiles for an enchanter's robe
> The eyed skin of a supple oncelot;
> And hath an ounce sleeker than youngling mole,
> A four-legged serpent he makes cower and couch,
> Now snarl, now hold its breath and mind his eye,
> And saith she is Miranda and my wife:
> 'Keeps for his Ariel a tall pouch-bill crane

He bids go wade for fish and straight disgorge;
Also a sea-beast, lumpish, which he snared,
Blinded the eyes of, and brought somewhat tame,
And split its toe-webs, and now pens the drudge
In a hole o' the rock and calls him Caliban;
A bitter heart that bides its time and bites.
'Plays thus at being Prosper in a way,
Taketh his mirth with make-believes: so He.

(ll. 150–69)

That lumpish sea-beast, "a bitter heart that bides its time and bites," is the tortured plaything of a sick child, embittered by having been cast out by a foster father. As a slave, Shakespeare's Caliban is rhetorically defiant, but his curses are his only weapon. Since he has not inherited his mother's powers, Caliban's curses are in vain, and yet they have the capacity to provoke Prospero and Miranda, as in the first scene where the three appear together:

PROSPERO: Come on,
    We'll visit Caliban my slave, who never
    Yields us kind answer.
MIRANDA: 'Tis a villain, sir,
    I do not love to look on.
PROSPERO: But as 'tis,
    We cannot miss him. He does make our fire,
    Fetch in our wood, and serves in offices
    That profit us. What ho! slave! Caliban!
    Thou earth, thou! speak.
CALIBAN: (*Within.*)   There's wood enough within.
PROSPERO: Come forth, I say, there's other business for thee.
    Come, thou tortoise, when?

Enter ARIEL *like a water-nymph.*

Fine apparition! My quaint Ariel,
Hark in thine ear.
ARIEL: My lord, it shall be done.   *Exit.*
PROSPERO: Thou poisonous slave, got by the devil himself
    Upon thy wicked dam, come forth!

Enter CALIBAN.

CALIBAN: As wicked dew as e'er my mother brush'd
    With raven's feather from unwholesome fen

Drop on you both! A south-west blow on ye,
And blister you all o'er!
PROSPERO: For this, be sure, to-night thou shalt have cramps,
Side-stitches, that shall pen thy breath up; urchins
Shall, for that vast of night that they may work,
All exercise on thee; thou shalt be pinch'd
As thick as honeycomb, each pinch more stinging
Than bees that made 'em.
CALIBAN: I must eat my dinner.
This island's mine by Sycorax my mother,
Which thou tak'st from me. When thou cam'st first,
Thou strok'st me and made much of me, wouldst give
     me
Water with berries in't, and teach me how
To name the bigger light, and how the less,
That burn by day and night; and then I lov'd thee
And show'd thee all the qualities o' th' isle,
The fresh springs, brine-pits, barren place and fertile.
Curs'd be I that did so! All the charms
Of Sycorax, toads, beetles, bats, light on you!
For I am all the subjects that you have,
Which first was mine own king; and here you sty me
In this hard rock, whiles you do keep from me
The rest o' th' island.
PROSPERO: Thou most lying slave,
Whom stripes may move, not kindness! I have us'd
     thee
(Filth as thou art) with human care, and lodg'd thee
In mine own cell, till thou didst seek to violate
The honor of my child.
CALIBAN: O ho, O ho, would't had been done!
Thou didst prevent me; I had peopled else
This isle with Calibans.
MIRANDA: Abhorred slave,
Which any print of goodness wilt not take,
Being capable of all ill! I pitied thee,
Took pains to make thee speak, taught thee each hour
One thing or other. When thou didst not, savage,
Know thine own meaning, but wouldst gabble like
A thing most brutish, I endow'd thy purposes
With words that made them known. But thy vild race

(Though thou didst learn) had that in't which
    good natures
Could not abide to be with; therefore wast thou
Deservedly confin'd into this rock,
Who hadst deserv'd more than a prison.
CALIBAN: You taught me language, and my profit on't
    Is, I know how to curse. The red-plague rid you
    For learning me your language!
PROSPERO: Hag-seed, hence!
    Fetch us in fuel, and be quick, thou'rt best,
    To answer other business. Shrug'st thou, malice?
    If thou neglect'st, or dost unwillingly
    What I command, I'll rack thee with old cramps,
    Fill all thy bones with aches, make thee roar
    That beasts shall tremble at thy din.
CALIBAN: No, pray thee.
    [*Aside.*] I must obey. His art is of such pow'r,
    It would control my dam's god, Setebos,
    And make a vassal of him.
PROSPERO: So, slave, hence!   *Exit Caliban.*
                                (1.2.307–74)

Is it, as some would say, that our resentment of Prospero and Miranda here and our sympathy (to a degree) with Caliban, are as irrelevant as a preference for Shylock over Portia? I do not think so, since Shylock is a grotesque bogeyman rather than an original representation, while Caliban, though grotesque, is immensely original. You can New Historicize Caliban if you wish, but a discourse on Caliban and the Bermudas trade is about as helpful as a neo-Marxist analysis of Falstaff and surplus value, or a Lacanian-feminist exegesis of the difference between Rosalind and Celia. Caliban's peculiar balance of character and personality is as unique as Falstaff's and Rosalind's, though far more difficult to describe. But Prospero's balance also yields reluctantly to our descriptions, as if more than his white magic is beyond us. Prospero never loses his anger or sense of outrage in regard to Caliban, and surely some guilt attaches to the magus, who sought to make Caliban into what he could not become and then went on punishing Caliban merely for being himself, Caliban, a man of his own island and its nature, and not at all a candidate for hermetic transformations. Caliban can be controlled and chastised by Prospero's magical art, but he is recalcitrant, and holds on to the strange dignity of being Caliban, although endlessly insulted by everyone who speaks to him in the play.

Alas, that dignity vanishes in the presence of the jester Trinculo and the drunken Stephano, with whom Caliban attempts to replace Prospero as master. The immense puzzle of Shakespeare's vision of Caliban is enhanced when the slave's most beautiful speech comes in the grotesque context of his seeking to soothe the fears of Trinculo and Stephano which are caused by the music of the invisible Ariel:

> Be not afeard, the isle is full of noises,
> Sounds, and sweet airs, that give delight and hurt not.
> Sometimes a thousand twangling instruments
> Will hum about mine ears; and sometime voices,
> That if I then had wak'd after long sleep,
> Will make me sleep again, and then in dreaming,
> The clouds methought would open, and show riches
> Ready to drop upon me, that when I wak'd
> I cried to dream again.
>
> (3.2.135–43)

This exquisite pathos is Caliban's finest moment, and exposes the sensibility that Prospero presumably hoped to develop, before Caliban's attempted rape of Miranda. The bitterest lines in the play come in Prospero's Jehovah-like reflections upon his fallen creature:

> A devil, a born devil, on whose nature
> Nurture can never stick; on whom my pains,
> Humanely taken, all, all lost, quite lost;
> And as with age his body uglier grows,
> So his mind cankers. I will plague them all,
> Even to roaring.
>
> (4.1.88–93)

This could be Milton's God, Schoolmaster of Souls, fulminating at the opening of *Paradise Lost*, book 3. True, Prospero turns to the rarer action of forgiveness and promises Caliban he yet will receive pardon and Caliban promises to "seek for grace." Yet Shakespeare was uninterested in defining that grace; he does not even tell us if Caliban will remain alone on the island in freedom, or whether he is to accompany Prospero to Milan, a weird prospect for the son of Sycorax. All that Prospero promises himself in Milan is a retirement "where / Every third thought shall be my grave." We want Caliban to be left behind in what is, after all, his own place, but Shakespeare neither indulges nor denies our desires. If Prospero is at last a kind of benign Iago (an impossible oxymoron), then Caliban's recalcitrances finally look like an idiosyncratic rebellion of actor against playwright, creature against demiurge. A warm monster is dramatically more sympathetic than a cold magus, but that simplistic difference does not explain away the enigma of Caliban. I suspect that Prospero forgives his enemies because he understands, better than we can, the mystery of time. His magic reduces to what Nietzsche called the will's revenge against time, and against time's "it was." Caliban, who need not fear time, and who hates Prospero's books of magic, perhaps represents finally time's revenge against all those who conjure with books.

Miraculous Harp: A Reading of Shakespeare's *Tempest*

Harry Berger, Jr.

In many of the later plays, some analogue of dramatic control is imposed—and conspicuously imposed—on action which would otherwise get out of control; action which indeed, in earlier tragedies, did get out of control. The echoes of, or allusions to, earlier tragic patterns in such plays as *Measure for Measure, Pericles, Cymbeline, The Winter's Tale,* and *The Tempest,* have often been remarked. The modes of resolution seem deliberately strained, unnatural, artificial, or unrealistic in these plays, especially since they resonate with allusions to earlier tragedies where resolutions were not forthcoming. This pattern tends to emphasize a crucial difference between life and theatre: in art, life's problems are displayed and then resolved, perhaps displayed in order to be resolved, perhaps resolved so that people can get up and go home. Yet on the other hand—and this distinguishes many of the later plays from the earlier festive comedies—neither characters nor spectators want to go home: sometimes this is because we are surprised by the unexpected and abrupt happy ending; sometimes because the play fading into a golden past makes us yearn after it; sometimes because the action is protracted, the ending delayed, by characters who seem reluctant to leave the play world and return to actuality. The plays often present themselves as temporary and all too fragile hiding places in, or from, the worsening world.

Such qualities of the last plays have evoked criticism of the sort leveled by Madeleine Doran at the earlier problem plays:

From *Shakespeare Studies* 5 (1969). © 1970 by the Center for Shakespeare Studies.

> They do not seem to us to be satisfactorily resolved in the con-
> ventional happy ending of comedy. . . . [and this is so] because
> of the working out of a serious moral problem in an action built
> of improbable device and lucky coincidence. The result is only
> too often to make the solutions seem trivial or forced.
>   The difficulty with these plays is that the problems are real-
> istically viewed, the endings are not. . . . the manipulation of
> intrigue and lucky chance to bring about the conventional happy
> ending gives the effect of an evasion of the serious moral issue
> the play.

The main difference between the problem plays and the last plays is that
in the latter not even the problems are realistically viewed: Shakespeare
would want us to distinguish the grim actuality of Vienna from the paste-
board villainies of Cymbeline's court. Though Professor Doran's remarks
are helpful as guides to description and interpretation, her intention to
criticize detracts from their value. The critical mood is wrong mainly because Shakespeare has anticipated her by building her criticisms into the
plays themselves. And in fact, the burden of the present essay will be to
suggest that Shakespeare would or could or did level Professor Doran's
criticism toward her own reading of *The Tempest:* "The action of the play
is Prospero's discovery to his enemies, their discovery of themselves, the
lovers' discovery of a new world of wonder, Prospero's own discovery of
an ethic of forgiveness, and the renunciation of his magical power." This
is, in epitome, perhaps the most commonly accepted view of the play, and
the best defense of this sentimental reading known to me has been made
by Stephen Orgel, who claims that from the first long dialogue with Miranda in 1.2, "Prospero's suffering . . . is essentially behind him," therefore
he "leads the play . . . through suffering to reconciliation and a new life."
Orgel goes on to cite the pattern of the masque of Ceres as evidence that
"the play is at this point moving away from the island and back to civilization": "The conclusion of the revels, the vision of the masque as an
'insubstantial pageant,' and all that that vision implies for Prospero, provide
a vital transition in the play to the renunciation of extraordinary powers
and the return to the ordinary world." Orgel admits that "the transition is
a painful one for Prospero," but his major emphasis is on the magician's
return, and on his preparing to reassume his old job.
    I find it hard to accept this reading as it stands, not because it is wrong,
but because it does not hit the play where it lives. The renunciation pattern
is *there,* but only as a general tendency against which the main thrust of the

play strains. There are too many cues and clues, too many quirky details, pointing in other directions, and critics have been able to make renunciation in this simple form the central action only by ignoring those details. Some of the puzzling items may be listed here: First, Prospero's language in describing the usurpation to Miranda, encourages us to believe that he is partly responsible for what happened, yet *he* never seems to take this into account; throughout the course of the play, he acts the part of the good man wronged by villains, and he is not above an occasional reference to his injured merit. Second, Gonzalo, for all his goodness, was in effect Antonio's accomplice; as Alonso's counselor he mitigated the harshness of Prospero's exile, but the fact remains that he was master of the design, responsible for its execution. Furthermore Gonzalo, for all his goodness, is just a bit of fool—maybe not as much as his knavish companions make him out to be, but a fool nonetheless. And yet the affinities between Gonzalo and Prospero are curiously insisted on in a number of verbal and ideological echoes. One more detail about Gonzalo: in any good romance his final speech would be the concluding sentiment; what ancient Gower is to *Pericles* Gonzalo would be to *The Tempest*; only it is not that kind of play, and his epilogue is badly timed, preceding the end by 113 lines.

Third: a very important set of questions emerging from the exposition in 1.2 have never, to my knowledge, been pursued: What are we really to do with Ariel, Sycorax, and Caliban? Why was Ariel punished by being stuck in a tree, why does he continually ask for his freedom, why the names *Sycorax* and *Caliban,* why the business about the witch's exile from Africa with its obvious echoes of Prospero's exile from Europe? What to make of a fact which many readers have noticed, the difference between Prospero's view of Caliban and ours? Why do we respond to certain qualities in Caliban which Prospero ignores, and why are we made to feel that the magician is more vindictive than he needs to be? Why the very full sense Shakespeare gives us of life on the island before the ship sailed in from Tunis, where Alonso had just married off his daughter Claribel to the Prince? In this connection, what are we to do with the odd set of references and allusions to Africa and Carthage, and especially to episodes from the first half of Virgil's *Aeneid?* These references prod us into remembering Aeneas's journey from Troy to Italy, from an old to a new world; they offer that journey as a shadowy resemblance to the various voyages and themes of the plot action, and they ask us to make some sense of the resemblance, or at least not to ignore it. Finally, why the twenty-line epilogue, in which Prospero asks the audience for applause, sympathy, and release?

The framework within which I shall consider these questions will be my disagreement with the sentimental reading I summarized earlier. The center of disagreement lies in the way I conceive the relation of Ariel and Caliban to Prospero. I want to begin, therefore, with something like an allegorical sketch of each of the first two characters.

II

To run through some preliminary and elemental distinctions, Ariel is air and fire to Caliban's earth and water. He is, in David William's words, " 'an airy spirit,' once imprisoned in a pine, and aspiring towards total liberty." Caliban, on the other hand, "is capable of not a few human conditions . . . so that his appearance, however brutal, must indicate an aspiration towards human nature, whereas Ariel's is away from it." Ariel's vision of freedom is to fly merrily after summer on the bat's back, and to live in the blossom that hangs on the bough; to spend his life far from the pains and labor of humanity, pleasuring himself in a green and garden world. He is not so much a spirit of nature as a spirit for nature. He looks forward to a time when the last vestiges of man will have enriched nature's strange treasuries and traceries, bones into coral and eyes into pearls. But Ariel is also gifted with magical powers, with theatrical and rhetorical talents. And though he demands his freedom, his powers are recreative in the sense that their exercise affords him delight. His last song—"where the bee sucks there suck I"—reminds me of Plato's familiar comparison of the poet to a honey-gathering bee in the garden of the muses. Like Plato's poet, Ariel is a winged thing whose art is magically inspired, therefore brought forth without labor. He bears a light and melodious burden, a far cry from firewood. As a figure of the idyllic fancy, he is at once pleasure-seeking and detached, a cool narcissist and a spirit of play. He plans to retire in a delicate and diminutive green world where he may compute his thyme among flowers, securely separated from the baser elements of man. He acknowledges as his own no things of darkness but owls and bats.

Ariel, then, is a recreative and self-delighting spirit whose art and magic are forms of play; a spirit freed by a magician whose presence on the island owes not a little to his own self-delighting recreative impulse, his own playing with arts and magic. Spirit and master have much in common: each has both a histrionic and a rhetorical bent which he delights to indulge, and each savors his performances to the full. In the case of Ariel, this is perhaps unambiguously clear only in his opening speech, but it is marked enough there to set up the analogy. Notice, in the following lines, how his obvious delight in magical performance is doubled by his pleasure in describing it, how his speech builds up to its final heroic period, changes from past tense to the more vivid present, and pushes beyond descriptive report to a high-toned epic personification. "Hast thou," asks Prospero, "*performed* to point the tempest that I bade thee?" And Ariel answers, "to every article":

> I boarded the King's ship: now on the beak,
> Now in the waist, the deck, in every cabin,
> I flamed amazement: sometime I'd divide
> And burn in many places; on the topmast,
> The yards, and boresprit would I flame distinctly,
> Then meet and join, Jove's lightnings, the precursors
> O' th' dreadful thunderclaps, more momentary
> And sight-outrunning were not. The fire and cracks
> Of sulphurous roaring the most mightly Neptune
> Seem to besiege and make his bold waves tremble;
> Yea, his dread trident shake.
>
> PROSPERO: My brave spirit!
>
> (1.2.193)

No doubt, as we learn a moment later, Ariel's enthusiasm owes something to his eagerness to get out from under and be free. Yet at the same time we respond to his gratuitous delight in putting on a good show and describing it in brave rhetoric. That this speaks to an answering delight in Prospero is evident throughout the play, most clearly in the two masques. At the end of the masque of judgment, he commends Ariel for performing "bravely the figure of this harpy," but also for following the script: "Of my instruction hast thou nothing bated / in what thou hadst to say" (3.3.86). And the script contains far more than is necessary to induce fear and contrition. As the majority of onstage responses indicate, it is for the most part a bravura display of hocus-pocus and spectacular effects mixed with a certain amount of learned allusion in the imitation and adaptation of the third *Aeneid*. John Cranford Adams remarks that Prospero did not *have* to be present up top throughout the show, and this only reinforces my feeling that he is there so that we can watch him enjoy his god's-eye view as he sees his work performed and observes the audience reaction;—a little like Tom Sawyer at his funeral. If he missed the first spectacle reported by Ariel, he is not going to miss this one.

In this connection, his way of announcing the wedding masque is a little odd:

> I must
> Bestow upon the eyes of this young couple
> Some vanity of mine Art: it is my promise,
> And they expect it from me.
>
> (4.1.39)

He says this to Ariel, who doesn't seem to have known about it before (and therefore answers, "Presently?"—"right away?"). He may well have promised it to Ferdinand and Miranda, but there is no previous mention of it. "Some vanity of mine Art," uttered after his previous *tours de force,* has about it a comic note of Chaucerian self-deprecation, stressed immediately by his sense of his own image—"I must live up to their expectations." Shortly after, when Ferdinand rises to the occasion by asking, "May I be bold / To think these spirits?" Prospero willingly explains, "Spirits, which by mine Art / I have from their confines call'd to enact / My present fancies" (4.1.119). The masque itself reveals much about his present fancies, and more is revealed by the very fact of its having been rather suddenly and gratuitously conceived.

Ariel and Prospero thus share a common delight in art which—in Prospero's case—continually distracts him from his ethical purpose, and in one famous instance leads him to forget what goes on around him. His ingenuous pleasure tends to make him sacrifice plot to spectacle, and drama to theater. David William remarks that "in no play is the visual trap more tempting or more dangerous," but he directs this criticism toward "producers [who] offer a visual accompaniment that more often than not distracts from the action instead of illuminating it." I think we can also read this as part of Shakespeare's portrayal of Prospero, a part intimately connected with the presence and meaning of Ariel, who—like Lear's fool—reflects his master's mind.

It may be pedantic to load theological symbolism onto the tree in which Ariel was trapped, but I shall do so for heuristic purposes, *viz.,* let Ariel trapped in the tree of fallen human nature (*in medio ligni*) be an emblem of Prospero's Milanese experience. From the beginning, the Duke's own airy-recreative impulse asserted claims that made him view his social and political circumstances as unduly burdensome. He neglected worldly ends for the seclusion in which he bettered his mind, made the liberal arts all his study, allowed himself to be transported and rapt in secret studies, claiming indeed that its very withdrawn exclusiveness made this study "o'erprize all popular rate." Thus he was easily deceived, betrayed, and exiled by the brother he trusted with "a confidence sans bounds," and to whom he committed his government. Prospero no less than Ariel might be deemed "a spirit too delicate / to enact . . . [the] earthy and abhorred commands," not of Sycorax, but of government in a world full of Antonios, Sebastians, and Alonsos. It may also be owing to Ariel that the ex-Duke of Milan has a fairly unhealthy attitude toward labor—toward good clean manual work. We hardly expect him, as an aristocrat, to wash his own dishes and light his own fires. But he seems to have an ethical as well as a practical and social aversion to labor: Caliban and Ferdinand do not simply do his chores for him; he makes it clear that they are doing it as punishment and as an ordeal of degradation. Work is the evil man's burden, and I find this cavalier attitude consonant with Prospero's general lack of interest in the active and common life, consonant also with his neoplatonic preference for the more refined labors of the contemplative life. For Prospero's secret study pretty clearly springs from and leads to a particular view of man. The curriculum consists of two courses, magic and liberal arts, a combination familiar to anyone acquainted with the optimism or meliorism of the Florentine Neo-platonists. The Duke of Milan may well have trusted his brother so much because his studies led him to envisage a brave new world peopled with noble creatures; a world purified of the baser strains of human nature, the more mundane problems of social order, which he seemed inclined to avoid. On the other hand, Prospero's boundless confidence and careless trust in Antonio suited his impulse to retirement. His ethical idealism and aesthetic or hedonistic idyllism tend to reinforce each other, tend in fact to converge.

As an emblem, the freeing of Ariel suggests that Prospero's exile had for him—whether or not he was aware of it—the character of a liberation. Alonso, Antonio, and Gonzalo simply accomplished on the level of external action what he would wish—what he already wished—for himself. He had renounced the dukedom in his mind before handing it over to Antonio. His being set adrift on the ocean, committed to a course which washed away the old burdensome world of civilization and translated him magically to a new world, unpeopled and unreal—this removal and isolation fulfill the process by externalizing his self-sufficient insularity. I think Shakespeare presents in Prospero the signs of an ancient and familiar psychological perplex connected with excessive idealism and the longing for the golden age; a state of mind based on unrealistic expectations; a mind therefore hesitant to look too closely at the world as it is. Under the pressure of actual life, so unguardedly sanguine a hope dialectically produces its op-posite, extreme disillusionment with things as they are. This in turn some-times leads to the violent repressiveness of iron-age justice, vaguely hinted at in Prospero's attitude toward Caliban; and it sometimes generates the wish to escape back into a paradisiac state of nature. Wish-fulfillment and nightmare are simple contraries, twinned and mutually intensifying im-pulses neither of which is more realistic than the other, both of which seize the mind they possess and carry it out of the world.

Freed from the mortal coil and body politic of Milan, the Ariel within Prospero finds and releases its double in the outside world. The fact that no one else knows of Ariel's existence testifies to the peculiar inwardness and privacy of Prospero. Ariel, the picture of Nobody, the secret who embodies Prospero's detachment and isolation, is his only confidante. And Ariel's persistent thrust toward absolute freedom from humanity exerts a corresponding pressure on Prospero. I read his desire for liberty as allegorically related to the central action of the play, Prospero's re-involvement with human beings after twelve years of magic for magic's sake. This action produces a conflict within the enchanter between his recreative and ethical, his egocentric and social, concerns—between the pleasure and power of his art on the one hand, and on the other, the claims of revenge or forgiveness, his obligations and privileges as a father, a fellow man, a ruler, and a victim. He feels the freedom of the inward Ariel jeopardized; he knows he cannot easily return while still possessing, or possessed by, a spirit which prefers coral to bones and pearls to eyes. Ariel's demands are therefore the other side of Prospero's decision to reenter the riven wood of humanity, and this decision is confirmed in action when Prospero splits the ship which will ultimately bear him to Milan. By the time of the epilogue, the two will have all but changed the places they occupied when Prospero first came to the island: Ariel will move from the tree trunk to his flowery Eden, Prospero from his magic hideaway to the bare platform surrounded on three sides by Englishmen—most of whom, we may imagine, might correspond to Trinculo's holiday fools who "will not give a doit to relieve a lame beggar," but "will lay out ten to see a dead Indian," and probably more to see a live savage.

Caliban and Sycorax throw another kind of light on Prospero. The name *Sycorax* means, among other things, *hooped together:* "with age and envy grown into a hoop," as Prospero says. Turned in upon herself with envy, raven-black with malice, exiled for "mischiefs manifold and sorceries terrible," she appears to be Prospero's antithesis—the nightmare which complements his wish-fulfillment—and this contrast is emphasized by their parallel situations. Both owe their banishment to motives which lead them to the study or practice of magic. Though Sycorax is motivated by pure evil, and Prospero's motives by contrast seem very good, both are equally antisocial, both have withdrawn into themselves, have proved unfit for, or inadequate to, social and political existence. If Prospero withdrew for traditional reasons—extreme idealism and idyllism, contemplation and recreation—Sycorax embodies some of the features of a contrary though equally traditional form of withdrawal: the plaintive withdrawal of the have-not, those figures of envy and malice whose dissatisfaction with their lot produces hatred of self and others; who long for the beauty they lack and hate it in others; who spend their time trying to violate others either to possess their beauty and otherness, or simply for the temporary relief and communion gained by seeing them suffer.

Something of this disposition has been transmitted to Caliban. To the familiar etymological interpretations of his name—*cannibal* and *blackness* (Romany, *cauliban*, E. K. Chambers)—I would add *Kali* (beauty) + *ban* or *bane,* and I would translate it in two ways: first, and most simply, "the bane of beauty," which is the way Prospero comes to see him. The second translation is a little more complicated, and it refers to what *we*—as opposed to Prospero— see in Caliban: "banned from beauty, beauty is his bane." Many critics have observed that he has areas of feeling and sensitivity of which Prospero is unaware. Stephen Orgel remarks on his rich fantasy and his concrete sense of the island's natural resources. Clifford Leech notes that although there is "no moral good in him," "Caliban speaks throughout the play in blank verse: he is aware of beauty, whether in Miranda or in the fair features of the island or in music or his dreams." But these aware-nesses lead only to frustration. And since he is only, so to speak, a first-generation human being, his desire apprehends limited forms of beauty—money, wine, woman, and song; his impulses to love and worship are moved by brave and fine appearances when they are not moved by mere alcohol and lust.

The important point to be made about Caliban is that he can by no means be reduced to a figure of pure evil, the antithesis of Miranda or Ariel, the counterpart of Antonio. His baseness is shot through with gleams of aspiration, though the mixture is unstable and the diverse motives often undifferentiated. He displays the most transcendent, the most poignant, and the most natural urges of man as well as the most foolish and murderous and disloyal. Critics have noted the persistent parallels between Caliban and Miranda in regard to the nature-nurture theme, but there is no reason why they stopped there. Situational parallels exist to Ferdinand (the logbearing), to Antonio (the plot), and to Prospero (who supplanted him on the island). His longings appear modulated into ideal civilized form in Miranda's ca-pacity for wonder and Ferdinand's for worshipful service; his visions of riches are sublimed in Prospero's insubstantial pageant and cloudcapped towers. Propero's original openness and subsequent antipathy to Antonio are reflected by both himself and Caliban in their island relationship. Finally, though it may seem odd, Caliban is not unlike Gonzalo in his attitude toward the island, and in the way his simpleminded good will is abused by Stephano and Trinculo (as Gonzalo's by Sebastian and Antonio). Child-like in his fears and passions, ingenuous in the immediacy of his responses to nature and man, open in the expression of feeling, Caliban at his most evil and traitorous shows up as a mere puppy, a comic Vice, a crude conspirator in the pointed contrast to Antonio established by their plots.

He is thus a moonlight distortion not only of the villains but of all the figures who have come to the island from the daylight world of civilization. In this sense he *stands for* the world; a handy and compact symbol of human nature, not as we know it, but as we might have found it at the beginning of time, in the pre-history of civilization, when Carthage, Tunis, and Troy were no more advanced than the Bermudas or Americas. We see in him all man's possibilities in their undeveloped form, and this means that we see the longing for brightness and beauty as no less real, no less rooted and persistent, than the tendency to darkness and evil. This is not what Prospero sees. Caliban is his epitome of human degradation: he is Milan without Prospero and Miranda; the cloven tree without Ariel; man as he really is and has become, rather than man as he could or should be—man, in short, as Antonio, spreading his poison from the top of civilized Italy down to its boot and root.

But Caliban in fact differs radically from his European counterpart. The difference is intimately bound up with the new world Prospero has created on the island, and to understand this we have to take very seriously Shakespeare's many efforts in the play to direct our glance backward to the history of the island before the play begins. This early history discloses an edifying transition from evil to good, and the emergence of a mythic or romance order. In his best of all impossible worlds, Prospero sees himself as the new god who has displaced the old, therefore the hero and savior as well as the king of his island universe. The only ripple of disorder is caused by a difference between the old and new generations of evil. Sycorax, who died before Prospero reached the island, belongs to the archetypal past and is therefore an absolute or pure figure of evil. She may also be Prospero's archetype, his figment of evil, a relief from the various shades of human gray in Europe. She was, or would have been, easy to identify as the enemy. There would have been no such complicating factors as love, or trust, or kinship, or hypocrisy. She could have been dealt with by force alone, and Caliban comforts us on this point by suggesting that Prospero's magic is stronger than his mother's. Thus no problem about Prospero's dealings with Caliban could develop were Caliban identical in these respects with Sycorax. What initially confused Prospero was the ambivalence and instability, the mixture of human motives we have already seen in Caliban. Unlike his mother, he offered Prospero a chance to exercise his more humane gifts in the liberal arts. When this failed, Prospero consigned him to the category of pure evil, alongside Sycorax and Antonio. The interesting thing about this whole episode is its resemblance to the Milanese experience, of which it is a modified repetition. Caliban claims that the island was taken from him by Prospero, and Prospero complains in return that he tried to be kind to Caliban, that he lodged him in his cell and gave him lessons. Like Hamlet's "Mousetrap," the situation admits of a certain amount of role-switching: either character in the island drama can be seen as playing both parts, loser and winner, in the Milanese coup. Caliban is "all the subjects that he (Prospero) has," and in kicking him about, Prospero may continually, and securely, reenact his failure in Milan. The analogy also points in the other direction: Prospero's ethical and symbolic reduction of Caliban to a figure of pure evil may suggest his share of guilt in encouraging Antonio to his crime; for unwittingly he did everything he could to cultivate whatever dram of evil his brother may have been heir to; in that sense, he—no less than Antonio—new-created the creatures that were his and gave them the occasion to say, with Caliban, "have a new master; get a new man."

The magic circle is a pastoral kingdom, a simplified and more controllable analogue of Prospero's former situation. To introduce some needless jargon, it is a version of what Erik Erikson calls the microsphere, "the small world of manageable toys" which the child establishes as a haven "to return to when he needs to overhaul his ego." There he constructs a model of his past painful experiences which will allow him to "play at doing something that was in reality done to him." In this way he "redeems his failures and strengthens his hopes" (*Childhood and Society*). The actual demands of Caliban's role in the mirosphere differentiate him from the civilized force of evil he symbolizes to Prospero. His value as a scapegoat exceeds his usefulness as a handyman. Continued in his helplessness, he stands as a token of his master's victory and power; continued in his boorish ingratitude, he is a constant reminder of Prospero's beneficence and patience. And to attenuate the tedium of the island's perfect bliss, his surliness no doubt gives Prospero a legitimate excuse for periodically venting his spleen and clearing his complexion. As a scapegoat and member of Prospero's microsphere, Caliban is bound by two basic conditions: First, he can always be controlled; this is of course guaranteed by the pleasant coupling of his general inefficiency with Prospero's magic. Second, so clear-cut a case of villainy sets Prospero's mind permanently at ease; there will be no deception, no misunderstanding of motives, no need to worry about Caliban's soul or conscience; he can be counted on to behave in a manner deserving only of righteous anger, discipline, and punishment. Poor Caliban is a platonist's black dream: Prospero feels he has only to lay eyes on his dark and disproportioned shape to know what Evil truly is, and where.

III

In William Strachey's letter describing and commenting on the 1609 Bermuda shipwreck and the expedition's subsequent fortunes in Virginia, there is a passage which supplies a close analogue to Prospero's experience with Caliban. Sir Thomas Gates, one of the leaders of the expedition, and Lieutenant Governor of the colony, had sent a man out on a mission, and the man was killed by Indians. Strachey reports that "it did not a little trouble the Lieutenant Governour, who since first landing in the Countrey . . . would not by any meanes be wrought to a violent proceeding against them, for all the practises of villany, with which they daily indangered our men; thinking it possible, by a more tractable course, to winne them to a better condition: but now being startled by this, he well perceived, how little a faire and noble intreatie workes upon a barbarous disposition, and therefore in some measure purposed to be revenged." Strachey's letter is dated 1610, and Shakespeare could have seen it in its unpublished form, but my interest is in something he could not have seen, a marginal comment in *Purchas His Pilgrimes* (1625), in which the letter was first published: "Can a Leopard change his spots? Can a Savage remayning a Savage be civill? Were not wee our selves made and not borne civill in our Progenitors dayes? and were not Caesars Britaines as brutish as Virginians? The Romane swords were best teachers of civilitie to this & other Countries neere us."

To this hard-headed historical perspective we may contrast another view of the—or *a*—New World, and a very different idea of the acquisition of civility. Imagine Prospero's delight were he to find himself translated to the island of Utopia where "the people are in general easygoing, good-tempered, ingenious, and leisure-loving. They patiently do their share of manual labor when occasion demands, though otherwise they are by no means fond of it. In their devotion to mental study they are unwearied . . . after a little progress, their diligence made us at once feel sure that our own diligence would not be bestowed in vain. They began so easily to imitate the shapes of the letters, so readily to pronounce the words, so quickly to learn by heart, and so faithfully to reproduce what they had learned that it was a perfect wonder to us" (Thomas More, *Utopia*). Here all things have been set in good order from the beginning. Within the scope of a single regime and lifetime, the first king "brought the rude and rustic people to such a perfection of culture and humanity as makes them now superior to all other mortals." In that island, which is Nowhere, Truth is not the daughter of Time. Time has no utility there, history no meaning. The hard-won accomplishments of western civilization have been handed to the Utopians in the Aldine edition, so that they can quickly and painlessly riffle through two thousand years of culture during study hour.

Shakespeare's image of unspoiled man lies somewhere between Prospero's view of him as a born devil and the vision Thomas More assigned to the professional traveller Raphael Hythloday (which means "well trained in nonsense"). But I think it is Hythloday's vision, rather than the more hard-headed attitude recorded by Purchas, which lurks behind Prospero's rejection. Prospero's phrase, "the dark backward and abysm of time," has a rich and profoundly resonant ring to us, but to him it signifies the space of twelve years, not the incredible vast of time which separates us from our progenitors. Shakespeare would have us remember that we cannot new-create Caliban from savagery to civility in twelve years, any more than we can new-create unregenerate Europeans in three hours, except in the world of romance.

The dark backward and abysm of time: Purchas gives us a better clue to its resonance than Hythloday or Prospero, and this clue is to be found in the dominant atmospheric effect of the play. Let me repeat David William's remark that Caliban's appearance "must indicate an aspiration towards human nature, whereas Ariel's is away from it." The two figures are separated by the whole of human history, civilization, and development. In Ariel alone, all calibanic urges except the desire of freedom have been transcended, sublimed away, become pure aesthetic play. Compressed into the insistently noted limits of an afternoon and a small island, are not only twelve years of experience, but the beginning and the end of civilized man, the new world and the old, Africa and Europe, the travels of Aeneas and those of Sir Thomas Gates, the golden age and an earnest of apocalypse. Similarly, our sense of spatial scale varies from the mini-world of elves and mushrooms through oceans and continents to the great globe itself; from unplummeted depths of earth and ocean through the green sea and cloud-capped towers toward the moon and the azure vault of heaven. The archaic world of folklore and superstition, the world of the mythy mind, is set beside the ultimate refinements of literary artifice, and the marvels of theatrical and hermetic thaumaturgy.

These spatial and temporal coordinates are significantly distinguished by the fact that Prospero is aware of the first but not of the second. Until he has bad dreams in the fourth act, his magic allows him to command infinite space while bounded in the nutshell of his microsphere. Yet his view into the distant past extends only half a generation. Milan seems long ago because he has spent his time in so different a world, and because there are no clocks on the island; in the romance milieu, it would make little difference whether Ariel howled away in his tree for one, twelve, or twelve hundred years. But there is another measure in the play which magnifies the dark backward and downward of time, a scale of which neither Prospero nor the other characters are seriously cognizant: We, however, may remember that Amphion's miraculous harp raised the Theban wall in the fabled age of gods and heroes; that in what seems like the dawn of history Dido came to Carthage from Phoenicia, and Aeneas relinquishing his first wife with his first civilization passed through Carthage on his way to Italy; that his settlement was to become the high and palmy state of Rome; that he abandoned his former home at the behest of the gods and for reasons of state; that the Trojans did not bring forth islands by sowing kernels in the sea—they ploughed the ocean to plant a difficult harvest they would not live to enjoy.

These echoes vibrate with the sense of history; they stretch out the expanse of time separating Caliban from the play's modern characters. And they provide us with a vantage point from which we may view with detachment as well as sympathy the turning point of the play—the moment during which Prospero suddenly recalls Caliban's conspiracy, interrupts the masque of Ceres, and delivers his elegy on the end of the revels and the end of the world.

The action beginning with the tempest and culminating in this moment saves Prospero from becoming, or rather remaining, another Raphael Hythloday. Until his disenchantment, he too fits the image of the colonizer as frustrated idealist, wishing for and therefore finding himself in a new world, unhampered by decadent fellow Europeans; eager to start over from the beginning and project a golden age of towers, palaces, temples, and theaters; a culture brought forth not through centuries of "sweat or endeavor," but like nature's foison, perhaps by "sowing kernels of it in the sea."

The source of his disenchantment is the same as the cause of his original abdication, and here again we find a close analogy in More's Utopia. Hythloday had also "devoted himself unreservedly to philosophy"; he had left his patrimony to his brothers and voyaged to the New World where, like Jaques in As You Like It, he begged to remain rather than return to the worldly stage. He considered service to king or commonwealth a futile disturbance of his own peace and quiet. More had lectured him on his disinterest and disillusion, saying, "If you cannot pluck up wrongheaded opinions by the root, if you cannot cure according to your heart's desire vices of long standing, yet you must not on that account desert the commonwealth. You must not abandon the ship in a storm because you cannot control the winds." This reproof follows the famous passage in which More criticizes Hythloday's Platonic disdain of the real world. Hythloday wants to free himself of the world because it neither listens nor lives up to his utopian philosophy: There is no room, More says, for the scholastic philosophy which would impose itself absolutely and rigidly on life's situations without regard to the needs, differences, and limits of particular contexts: "But there is another philosophy, more practical for statesmen, which knows its stage, adapts itself to the play in hand, and performs its role neatly and appropriately. This is the philosophy you must employ. . . . Would it not . . . [be] preferable to take a part without words than by reciting something inappropriate to make a hodgepodge of comedy and tragedy? You would have spoiled and upset the actual play by bringing in irrelevant matter—even if your contribution would have been superior in itself. Whatever play is being performed, perform it as best you can, and do not upset it all simply because you think of another which has more interest."

Prospero thought of another play. In this, he and Hythloday differ from the old counsellor Gonzalo. Gonzalo performs the play in hand as well as he can, but not quite well enough. He is very much the man Hythloday refuses to be, the well-intentioned advisor who remains haplessly in the world. He believes in, or at least clings to, the happy solutions wherever they may be found; he tries to ease matters when it is possible to do so without causing trouble. Shakespeare places in his mouth the famous if muddled speech about the golden age (some of it borrowed from Montaigne's essay on the cannibals), and even though Gonzalo claims he uttered it merely to make the king feel better, it accords with the sentiments he expresses elsewhere in the play. "Had I plantation of this isle . . . and were [I] the King on it" I would admit "no kind of traffic,"

> no name of magistrate;
> Letters should not be known; riches, poverty,
> And use of service, none; contract, succession,
> Bourn, bound of land, tilth, vineyard, none;
> No use of metal, corn, or wine, or oil;
> No occupation; all men idle, all;
> And women too, but innocent and pure;
> No sovereignty;—

SEBASTIAN:　　　　　　　　Yet he would be King on 't.

> ANTONIO: The latter end of his commonwealth forgets the
>   beginning.
> GONZALO: All things in common Nature should produce
>   Without sweat or endeavor: treason, felony,
>   Sword, pike, knife, gun, or need of any engine,
>   Would I not have; but Nature should bring forth,
>   Of its own kind, all foison, all abundance,
>   To feed my innocent people. . . .
>   I would with such perfection govern . . .
>   T' excel the Golden Age.
>
>   (2.1.139–64)

This kind of pastoral wish-fulfillment was a cliché in Shakespeare's time—getting rid of all problems by getting rid of civilization, throwing the baby out with the bath, letting Nature and the gods do with greater ease and certainty what men try to do and always bungle. The interesting thing is that the speech is echoed in some of the significant details and themes of Prospero's masque of Ceres, put on in act 4 as a betrothal celebration for the benefit of Ferdinand and Miranda. Gonzalo's speech is simple and simpleminded, direct and unreflective, inconsistent but well-intentioned. Prospero's masque is a very artful, sophisticated and refined—not to mention magically induced—expression of the same pastoral escapism. The affinities between counsellor and magician are stressed in a number of ways: First, Prospero is obviously fond of Gonzalo. Second, both assume that the masque of judgment has produced the desired feelings of contrition in Alonso, Sebastian, and Antonio, though we see nothing in the sinners' behavior to justify this assumption. Third, both seem to have suppressed or ignored the question of their own contribution to the Milanese coup. Both characters thus share equally in a refusal to look too closely at the actual state of affairs, and more generally, at the world they live in.

But here the resemblance stops. The same attitude which is high-strung, sharply pitched, in Prospero, is loose and jangly in Gonzalo, who is marked by a certain intellectual and moral slackness. What Gonzalo naively accepts, Prospero tries to re-create by his art; he has come during the course of the action to suspect that this is the only way in which things can be made to happen as he would like them to happen. Gonzalo expresses and embodies the attitude Prospero left behind him, the other side of romance from disenchantment. As he favors Gonzalo, so he clings to the sentimental attitude he no longer believes, and tries briefly to evoke it by the techniques of magic and theater. Gonzalo's closing speech is in fact a statement of the usual sentimental reading of The Tempest:

> O, rejoice
> Beyond a common joy, and set it down,
> With gold on lasting pillars: in one voyage
> Did Claribel her husband find at Tunis,
> And Ferdinand her brother found a wife
> Where he himself was lost; Prospero his dukedom
> In a poor isle; and all of us ourselves
> When no man was his own.
>
> (5.1.206–13)

To which we may imagine Prospero's unheard reply: " 'Tis so to thee."

In one respect, the two characters are diametrically opposed: In my ideal kingdom, Gonzalo affirms, "letters should not be known," and this bears out our own suspicion about his literacy. His knowledge of the classics is a little shaky, and Antonio justifiably refers to him as "a lord of weak remembrance." He confuses Carthage with Tunis, and tries to console Alonso by comparing Claribel to the notable Carthaginian widow and suicide. "His word," Antonio jeers, "is more than the miraculous harp" of Amphion, who raised the walls of Thebes by music. And then he and Sebastian finish poor Gonzalo off:

SEBASTIAN: He hath rais'd the wall, and houses too.
ANTONIO: What impossible matter will he make easy next?
SEBASTIAN: I think he will carry this island home in his pocket,
  and give it his son for an apple.
ANTONIO: And sowing the kernels of it in the sea, bring forth
  more islands.

More than the miraculous harp: in a way, the last laugh is on Antonio, since his own plans are about to be foiled by something like a miraculous harp. But the phrase ripples outward beyond its context. It is the harp of convenient forgetfulness and the sweet air of fantasy rearranging history, fact, and life, to accord with one's wish. And it is also the miraculous harp of romance and magic, theater and art, raising Gonzalo's untutored hopes and evasions to the level of man's highest accomplishments; raising within the brief compass of island and stage, the brief space between afternoon storm and dinner, the wall, the houses, the towers, palaces and temples, of the great globe new-created.

The opposing music, the resonance which makes *The Tempest* more (that is, less) than the miraculous harp, is heard most clearly in the Virgilian echoes which are thrown away by the flippancy of the ignorant villains no less than by the happy vagueness of Gonzalo. The way of Virgil and of

Thomas More is felt in the specter of Aeneas who played the part handed him by the gods, from the chaos of his first tempest through the threats and temptations of Celaeno and Dido to the final victory, if one can call it that, over Turnus. The endurance of Aeneas suggests something also about the endurance of civilization, especially when we place his encounter with the Italic New World beside the play's image of the American New World. The presence in *The Tempest* of Troy, Italy, and Bermuda, provides a sense of rhythmic recurrence, a ground bass to the elegiac burden of the revels speech. There will always be new worlds both behind us and ahead of us, and it is not likely that the work of twelve years or three hours will finally jeopardize the good, or uproot the evil of the ancient globe we inherit and transmit.

Yet on the other hand, the Virgilian echoes do establish a measure of the condition of present-day Naples, once part of Aeneas's new world. Alonso left Naples to marry his apparently unwilling daughter Claribel to the Prince of Tunis. For reasons which strike me as worth looking into, but which I have not yet been able to puzzle out, Africa has lost a Sycorax and gained a Claribel. Claribel's pale romance name pushes her toward the status of a personification, and if we put this together with the questionable nature of the marriage, the oddly inappropriate analogy to the widow Dido, and the confusion of Tunis with Carthage, we may be willing to entertain one more allegorical fantasy, in which Alonso's voyage is a reflection of his state: the civilized European soul compromising with darkness, surrendering its clear-beautiful ideals for the sake of expediency, and thereby reversing the forward direction of western man's arduous Virgilian journey. The voyage does not begin but ends, at least temporarily, with a Virgilian storm, and the angry divinity is not Juno but Prospero.

IV

Prospero's twelve years of romance, following Ariel's release from the cloven tree, seem to have consisted mainly of shadow boxing. Perhaps by the time he releases the Italians from the cloven ship, he is ready for a real enemy. During the early scenes he is clearly intent on, and excited by his project. He has already made and confirmed his decision in raising the tempest; and in his speeches to Miranda, Ariel, and Caliban, he seems on the verge of packing. In all three interchanges he has the air at once of summarizing the past and looking toward the future. And one of his chief concerns is to impress his image on his auditors. "Look what they have done to us," he says to Miranda. "Beware of my power and remember what you owe me," he says to Ariel and Caliban. Staging himself in roles designed to evoke sympathy, fear, or guilt; working on them by rhetoric rather than by magic; reviewing the past to place it in clear perspective: these aspects of his behavior reveal Prospero going through a test run, a dress rehearsal, preparatory to his confrontation with Alonso and Antonio.

As he moves from Miranda to Ariel to Caliban, his tone and bearing undergo significant changes. He is least easy and assured with Miranda, most with Caliban. It seems harder for him to deal, or know how to deal, with the daughter he loves than with his pet monster. He chooses his words very carefully; his sentences are at first disordered, his thoughts rambling, his narrative hesitant and digressive. Only gradually and with effort does he find the didactic handle, and gain confidence that he is producing the desired effect. To evoke the proper moral feelings in Miranda, he presents the past as a didactic romance, a parable of good and evil brothers. The interjections with which he punctuates his story—his "attend's" and "mark me's"—serve in every case to underline Antonio's perfidy. At the same time, they betray a certain rhetorical nervousness: he wants to make sure he is getting his message across. This is apparently not the sort of thing he has had much practice in during the last twelve years.

The homiletic impulse gains force with Ariel, to whom he speaks in terms of hellfire, purgatory, and redemption, using—or rather creating— the pretense that Ariel has forgotten the causes and nature of his debt to Prospero. Critics have mistakenly assumed that Prospero is angry in this scene. No doubt he feels some impatience at first, since Ariel's demand for freedom delays his project. But he immediately warms to the chance to stage himself in a moralizing vein, and I think he relishes the display of righteous anger through which he dramatizes for Ariel the latter's ingratitude and his own Powerful Goodness. This is characteristic of Prospero as of other Shakespearean figures: his delight in the present moment of playing, speaking, or performing, distracts him from his larger purpose, leads him momentarily to digress and indulge the immediate impulse. The pleasure of his little scene with Ariel gives him the idea of trying a repeat performance on wretched Caliban. Clifford Leech, who is not overly fond of Prospero, amusingly points up this motive: "After he has told Miranda his story and given Ariel his instructions and his morning lesson in obedience, he awakens Miranda . . . and oddly suggests: 'We'll visit Caliban my slave, who never / Yields us kind answer,' Miranda is reluctant to join in this kind of sport, but she is easily overridden." Prospero has already settled Caliban's ethical hash, and knows that he is a much better prospect for the role of ingrate than Ariel, whom he had to interrupt in order to keep him from yielding a number of kind answers not in the script. In contrast to his arduous effort with Miranda, the dialogue or flyting match with Caliban is released like a coiled spring.

These very different styles of behavior evoked by Miranda and Caliban establish the problem of the play. Even as he begins to set his plot machinery in motion, he is confronted by two alternatives: In consoling Miranda over the shipwreck, he says, "I have done nothing but in care of thee." The implications of this care reach beyond Ferdinand to Naples and Alonso. If he is going to do right by Miranda as well as himself, it will not be enough to discipline Ferdinand, to save the younger generation while their elders sink in the slough. The more difficult and humane course entails reconciliation with Alonso, but this would in itself be hollow unless preceded by "heart's sorrow / And a clear life ensuing" on the king's part. And since Antonio now infects Alonso's presence, Prospero perhaps hopes that he may influence even him to repent. In this way he might make all of them find themselves "when no man was his own," and he might restore the world to that brave and new condition he seems to have implanted as a prospect in Miranda's mind. This, I think, is one alternative, the favored one, entertained by Prospero. It is involved with his concern for Miranda and her future, it demands a delicacy and tact he he has not had to exercise for years (if ever), and its various issues are by no means easily predictable. The other and much simpler alternative, suggested by Caliban, is vengeance, discipline, servitude, and liberal doses of magic. The choice is complicated by Prospero's interest in putting on impromptu amateur theatricals. He is obviously more at home in roles allowing him to cleave the ear with horrid speech, make mad the guilty and appall the free. All these pressures are at work in the last part of 1.2, the scene with Ferdinand. His eagerness to unite Alonso's son with Miranda is balanced by his natural desire to try Ferdinand and assess his quality (to make the swift business uneasy). But the balance is upset by the carryover of the theatrical anger generated in the previous scenes with Ariel and Caliban. The situation is at once funny and a little unpleasant: Miranda puzzled and upset, Ferdinand confounded, Prospero carried away by the chance to play at being the local constabulary, all the while chortling happy asides to Ariel and to himself. The scene reveals the extent to which his reliance on his various arts allies itself with his tendency to swerve toward the easier alternative. His use of theatrical indirections—eavesdropping, role-playing, hiding his true feelings from others—is intimately connected with his habitual isolation, his aversion to social intercourse and consequent inexperience in dealing with others. He seems reluctant to confront people directly, to trust his spontaneous reflexes or commit himself to the normal channels of communication.

And yet I think that at the outset he would prefer the more difficult alternative, Miranda's way not Caliban's. He would like to undo Antonio's evil and new-create the others by making them feel the inward pinches of conscience, rather than—as with Caliban—the merely physical pinches inflicted by his spirits. He would like to awaken and quicken them to their stagnancy, their ebbing reason mudded in spiritual ooze, so that the cleansing tide will return and purge them of their foul weather. This, rather than dunk them by magic force in some filthy mantled horse-pond, and send them off punished, impressed by his power, but otherwise unchanged—like Caliban, who leaves the stage muttering a travesty of the sentiment Prospero would like to hear: "I'll be wise hereafter, / And sue for grace."

What happens to Prospero's intentions during the play is a modified repetition of what happened when he swerved from Miranda through Ariel to Caliban in 1.2.; and of what happened after he tried to deal humanely with Caliban; and of what happened after he entrusted Milan to Antonio. Only this time the effect cuts much deeper. For of all Shakespeare's human characters he is the only one to have become a god of power, to have attained to Hamlet's kingdom of infinite space in the nutshell of his microsphere, to have entered and passed through pure romance, to have achieved the dearest wish of hermetic sage or mage. His must therefore be the greatest disenchantment. He finds that magic cannot save souls, cannot even pinch the will. More than this, he finds that magic is the only effective policeman, and perhaps he comes to feel that there is very little to look forward to in a world without magic, the world to which he has committed himself to return. This mood has been well described in a recent study by Robert Hunter, who discussed the play's insistence on the inveteracy, the indestructibility of evil. "Only a rigid and unceasing control of the sort that Prospero had exercised over Caliban and . . . Antonio, can keep good in its . . . ascendancy." Prospero's pardoning of Antonio lacks any feeling, Hunter observes, because he knows that "to forgive unregenerate evil is safe only when . . . the good are in firm and undeceived control." But *control* here should be understood in a more restrictive sense than Hunter intends it; it is a control exerted nowhere but in the never-never land of magic and romance. This is why Prospero connects despair to his lack of "spirits to enforce, art to enchant," in the epilogue.

Caliban's role and function in this process are peculiar. As a model and scapegoat, everything that rendered him psychologically useful in the microsphere contributes to Prospero's disenchantment during the course of the play. The reduction of Caliban or man to a devil was the easier way out when Prospero wanted to resolve his mind, protect himself from humane attachments, maintain his psychic distance and mastery in his withdrawn world; but it is no help when he is preparing himself to return. Caliban's ineffectiveness now sets him apart from evil man and links him more closely to those ideal conditions of the microsphere which Prospero is about to renounce—there are, after all, no mooncalves in Milan. I can see no evidence for the view that Caliban is a real threat who keeps Prospero on edge, nor for the pietistic reading of the subplot as moral parody—e.g., the idea that Caliban's plot to murder Prospero as a comic analogue to the crimes of Alonso, Antonio, and Sebastian reduces the pretensions of the latter by comparing their behavior "to the deformed and drunken idiocies of the clowns" (Hunter). On the contrary, the analogy stresses the difference between the unreal symbol and what it represents—between the comic helplessness to which Prospero has reduced his symbol, and the insidious craft which would have succeeded anywhere but on the island. It is only in respect of the rootedness of evil that symbol and referent, Caliban and Antonio, coincide. And it is the awareness of this concidence, intensifying through the play since the murder attempt in the second act, which is surely on Prospero's mind when Ariel tells him that the three drunkards are "bending toward their project." "A devil," he exclaims, "a born devil, on whose nature / Nurture can never stick: on whom my pains, / Humanely taken, all, all lost, quite lost!" He is deeply troubled, as Ferdinand and Miranda had noticed, but this has nothing to do with the external plot, the threat on his life, such as it is.

He is troubled because at this moment the meaning he has read into Caliban, and the way represented by Caliban, become for him the meaning and the way of reality. The series of reenactments of the same pattern of betrayal persuades him to generalize and validate his disillusion as the one abiding truth of life. The radical persistence of evil which he validates for himself at this moment is only the objective consequence of another persistence—his idealistic separation of Ariel from Caliban; of Ariel from the cloven tree; of liberal arts from servile labor; of the vanished age of gold which must be restored, from the present age of iron which must be either repressively disciplined or willfully ignored. The implied validation of Caliban as the real model of man is matched by the equally hasty act of generalization which connects the dissolving masque, first to a dissolving culture, then to a dissolving world. I think we are meant to note the suddenness, the violence and facility, with which this reversal of his divided values takes place. What he feels this time, and for the first time, is that everything golden, noble, beautiful, and good—the works of man, the liberal arts, the aspirations variously incarnated in towers, palaces, temples, and theaters—that all these are insubstantial and unreal compared to the baseness of man's old stock. And not merely as vanities; but as deceptions, fantasies which lure the mind to escape from its true knowledge of darkness and which, dissolving, leave it more exposed, more susceptible, more disenchanted than before.

Here and now, Caliban becomes most truly Prospero's bane of beauty, the catalyst leading him, in his revels speech, to criticize as groundless the arts and projects, the beliefs and hopes by which he had ordered his life. The crux of his self-criticism lies in the phrase, "the baseless fabric of this vision," and especially in the word *baseless*. *Baseless* means two things: insubstantial, not firmly based, without proper grounds; but also, not base, not evil, too purely beautiful, excluding the dark substance of man; therefore, once again, without grounds. "We are such stuff / As dreams are made on—*on* as well as *of*: the evil matter or basis, the Calibanic foundation on which our nobler works are built, which they deceptively cover over, or from which they rise as in escape. Prospero would say, as Spenser said of the golden House of Pride, "full great pittie, that so faire a mould / Did on so weake foundation ever sit" (*The Faerie Queene*, 1.4.5). And man's works are dreams not only in being vanities, fragile illusions, but also in being—as Freud called them—the guardians of sleep protecting the mind in its denial of or flight from reality. Feeling this, Prospero might well envy his actors for being spirits who can melt into thin air after their performance. The best the vexed and aging mortal creature can hope for is to have his little life rounded—*crowned*—with sleep.

The perspective of the revels speech is itself a form of escape from mortality. It is the god's-eye view and therefore identical to that which dominated the masque of Ceres, even though the content of the masque was pastoral and that of the revels speech heroic. Pastoral and heroic perspectives may be used indifferently, as here, to distance or diminish the immediate problems of real life. The masque is in every respect an exorcism of evil. It was arbitrarily introduced as a distraction, a vanity of Prospero's art. "Some vanity of mine art" (4.1.41) is meant to sound self-deprecating: "Just a little something extra, and I'm only doing it because they expect it of me." But it also sounds apologetic, for he is asking Ariel to bear with him while he puts on one more show, and the revels speech shows him to have become aware of his self-indulgence. At any rate, his spirits enact his "present fancies," and thus reveal the state and tendency of his mind: by incantation and evocation they dispel not only the foul plot but also the thoughts of lust, intemperance, and disloyalty which had occupied him in his previous conversation with Ferdinand and Miranda.

Stephen Orgel speaks of the masque as a boundary leading the play from nature back to society, but this is almost certainly inaccurate: The masque pictures an idyllic nature, winterless, moving directly from harvest to spring. It begins when Iris calls Ceres away from a less ideal and very English nature whose character—"thy sea-marge, sterile and rocky-hard"—communicates itself to the conventional woes imposed on lasslorn bachelors by cold nymphs crowned for chastity (4.1.64–69)—as if Prospero sees only untempered chastity or intemperate lust, one or another kind of nunnery, possible in the actual world; the extremes may be tempered nowhere but on the magic island and in the masque where love is guided by gods. Married fertility is praised on the model of the securely determined round of nature. The imagery of this improved cycle seems to me a deliberately simplified and purged image of the human contract it celebrates, for it avoids those very problems of trust and self-discipline which Prospero himself had earlier raised with Ferdinand. At the same time the more unpleasant themes on Prospero's mind resonate even in their exclusion: The possibilities fulfilled in the fourth *Aeneid* are carefully exorcised (4.1.87–101), though just as carefully mentioned. Iris, announcing Juno's command to the Naiads, "temperate nymphs" of "windring brooks," warns them to "be not too late." The celebration of married sex is depicted by a conventional image of harvest dancing, yet even in their displacement to natural and collective activity, the details echo Prospero's concerns: "You sunburned sicklemen, of August weary, / Come hither from the furrow and be merry" (4.1.134–35). The passage of time, the brevity of holiday, the weariness of laborers, and the sexual associations, all press into the couplet. Finally, Prospero's desire to protract the entertainment and delay the return to actuality, is evident in the rhetoric of the masque, with its catalogues, its clustering adjectives, its appositions, and its "windring" sentences. The masque is thus a brief withdrawal into the golden age, Gonzalo's dream as magical theater, yet the realities of life which it evades are woven into its texture, revealing those pressures which now distract Prospero and become explicit in the revels speech.

The play does not end with the revels speech, however, any more than the epilogue ends with the word *despair*. The consequences of this private recognition scene are very odd. In fact there do not seem to be any consequences at first. Caliban and his new friends come onstage, freshly pickled and following Ariel's display of "glistering apparel." Caliban is here at his most cunning and Antonine. But shortly after, the plotters are put to rout. Prospero, to quote Leech once more, "turns his canine spirits on Caliban and his companions" and "bids Ariel see that the tormenting is done soundly." It clearly relieves him from his attack of *Weltschmerz* to get back into the role of punishing magician and have his egregious culprit handy. But Ariel's description of the plotters preceding their arrival onstage had made them look like helpless idiots, unworthy of Prospero's fury. No such anger or vengeance is directed toward Antonio, and I think the reason for this is Prospero's deeper sense of the futility of such responses rather than his more humane intentions where evil men are concerned. With Caliban, he retreats temporarily into the microsphere, where punishment had therapeutic value, and relieves himself once more at the expense of his scapegoat. The exigencies of the subplot, the demands of immediate physical danger, the rewards of an immediate physical solution, the panacea of magic: all these are now a positive diversion because they have so little relation or correspondence to the subtler and less effective, the more difficult and less satisfying modes of activity to be encountered in the macrosphere.

The diversion continues on another and more significant level in act 5, during which he relies heavily on magic and spectacle, giving free expression to his love of theatrical display. Act 4 concludes with Prospero in better spirits. "At this hour," he crows, "lie at my mercy all mine enemies." In this mood he retires, and emerges to open the fifth act in the same frame of mind, but all dressed up in his magic robes: "Now does my project gather to a head, / My charms crack not, my spirits obey, and time / Goes upright in his carriage." The words have the ring of incantatory self-persuasion. No doubt he feels to some extent the exhilarated sense of approaching triumph, but he is also intent on keeping himself keyed up for the performance which lies ahead.

Ariel reports that the king, Sebastian, and Antonio, "abide all three distracted, / And the remainder mourning over them," but chiefly good old Gonzalo, whose "tears run down his beard." It is important to notice just how much or little Ariel says here. "Your charm," he continues, "so strongly works 'em, / That if you now beheld them, your affections / Would become tender":

PROSPERO: Dost thou think so, spirit?
ARIEL: Mine would, sir, were I human.
PROSPERO: And mine shall.
　　Hast thou, which art but air, a touch, a feeling
　　Of their afflictions, and shall not myself,
　　One of their kind . . . be kindlier moved than thou art?
　　Though with their high wrongs I am struck to th' quick,
　　Yet with my nobler reason 'gainst my fury
　　Do I take part. The rarer action is
　　In virtue than in vengeance. They being penitent,

> The sole drift of my purpose doth extend
> Not a frown further. Go, release them, Ariel.
> My charms I'll break, their senses I'll restore,
> And they shall be themselves.
>
> (5.1.18)

Ariel has said nothing about their being penitent; he said they were distracted, that is, enchanted, which made the others, chiefly Gonzalo, "brimful of sorrow and dismay." His phrase, "your charm so strongly works 'em," may suggest the inner effect on their souls, but Ariel's context throughout is visual, and seems to mean, "if you saw how terribly uncomfortable and helpless they appeared, and if you saw how sorry this made the others, you would have pity on them." (*Them* may refer to Gonzalo and the rest of the entourage as well as the distracted trio.) So far as we know, only Alonso has displayed anything resembling remorse, and this is by no means clear: his final words in the masque of judgment scene suggest that he feels himself involved in some kind of retributive action connected with Prospero's old grievance, an action which has taken his son from him and which therefore impels him, in his grief for Ferdinand, to contemplate suicide. Sebastian and Antonio respond to the masque with two lines of foolish bravado before leaving the stage, and it is Gonzalo who makes the interpretation preferred by Prospero: "All three of them are desperate," he says; "their great guilt, / Like poison given to work a great time after, / Now gins to bite the spirits" (3.3.104). In view of what we have just seen, I do not think this is, or is meant to be, an accurate inference. It is of a piece with Gonzalo's other perceptions and judgments on the island, and I think it conveys more information about him than about his companions.

Prospero's "they being penitent" is also an unwarranted inference which tells us less about the inner state of his enemies than about the state he wants to produce in them by his magical spectacles and illusions. The masque of judgment, with Prospero occupying the god's position on top, was intended not simply to offer his courtly spectators roles, like an ordinary masque, but to assign them changes of heart, to catch their consciences. It was his major attempt to follow Miranda's alternative. And in the present speech, Prospero is not considering a change of heart in himself, but a change, a slight adjustment, of role which will make his part in the recognition scene more effective. Thus the deliberate and detached tone of the phrase, "with my nobler reason 'gainst my fury / Do I take part," suggests to me that he is selecting, rather than experiencing, his response. And the next statement is not so much a sententious commonplace as it is the critical musing of an artist or playwright aiming at the right touch: "The rarer action is / In virtue than in vengeance." The sentiment accords with his deeper feeling that both vengeance and forgiveness are futile, but his attention here is to the dramatic moment: it will make a better effect, because unexpected, if he reacts to their contrition with a display of divine forbearance, if he shows himself trying to fight down his just anger and offer them more leniency than they deserve. Therefore—and he is still thinking of theatrical effects—"therefore, not a *frown* further." Throughout the speech he holds his image at arm's length to apply the finishing touches before going onstage.

He does not go onstage, however, until he has delayed the action once again in the nostalgic summary of past magical achievements over which he lingers before threatening to drown his book (5.1.33–57). As the speech dramatizes his growing reluctance to rejoin humanity, so the rough magic he fondly recalls was practiced in a world devoid of any other human presence. The use of pastoral and heroic perspectives which characterized the masque of Ceres and the revels speech is repeated here: His former playgrounds were scaled to sub- and superhuman dimensions: the world of elfin pastoral and the cosmic arena where he played a game which anticipated Milton's War in Heaven. His elves rejoice to hear the curfew, they work when people sleep, and they leave the sands printless. These insubstantial spirits were his assistants, his "weak masters," in staging wars fought not by men or angels, but by the elements in the empty space "twixt the green sea and azure vault." The two details which do not square with the desert island locale are both relevant to his preference for a world without living or conscious men: the solemn curfew, and the graves which Prospero commanded to open. And the remark about the elves who "chase the ebbing Neptune, and to fly him / When he comes back" (5.1.35–36) is oddly echoed forty-five lines later, when he observes that his charmed victims are returning to their senses:

> Their understanding
> Begins to swell, and the approaching tide
> Will shortly fill the reasonable shore,
> That now lies foul and muddy.
>
> (5.1.79–82)

The elfin instruments of his magic will fly the swelling tide of reason in a more permanent manner, when the world of ordinary daylight and common recognition returns. And as far as Prospero is concerned, it would be better if the sinners could remain asleep; in restoring them to their sinful waking selves, he forces himself away from the magic island and closer to the real world.

Two interrelated factors contribute to his growing pessimism about human nature and his increasing reluctance to abjure his self-delighting magical existence: (1) With the exception of Alonso, none of the characters undergoes substantive changes as a result of Prospero's actions. Neither Antonio nor Sebastian gives any sign of remorse. Ariel's efforts to please his master spring, in spite of Prospero's affection for him, chiefly from his eagerness to be free. (2) I think we are meant to notice that he displays a limited knowledge of human nature. This is most evident in relation to Miranda and Ferdinand. They are so obviously pure and good, so obviously literary stereotypes of youthful love and virtue, that his "trials" of Ferdinand's love, and his warning about temperance, seem excessive and unnecessary. The trial itself is peculiar: it amounts to proving oneself a true and faithful lover by carrying some thousand logs of wood and not behaving like Caliban in the process. We may justify Prospero's obtuseness in discerning or trusting apparent virtue on the grounds of his own betrayal of Antonio. But there is a more general reason, which is simply that "the liberal arts," not people, politics, or society, were all his study. Neglecting worldly ends for the seclusion in which he bettered his mind, how could he be expected to have normal acquaintance with concrete human motives, character, and behavior? Like the Duke of Vienna, he seems to have been incapable of coping with, much less ruling, his fellow men in the normal ways and in direct encounter.

His inwardness and privacy are sustained throughtout the play. We hardly ever see him engage others in the easy or open way of friendship. I do not mean this statement to be understood in the context of actual life, which would make such an observation ridiculous. Rather I have in mind the relations of other Shakespearean heroes to their fellows. Most of them have at least one companion whom they love, or trust, or with whom they deal openly, very often the opposing voice or foil which Maynard Mack has remarked as a characteristic feature of the tragedies. Prospero is much more the Complete Loner than these heroes, closer in this respect to the wicked characters who keep their own counsel. He combines typical motives of the magician and the actor: Like the first, he prefers the security of the one-way window relationship in which he may observe without being observed, and may work on others from a distance. Like the second his reticence to expose himself in spontaneous or unguarded dealings blends with a love of the limelight, a delight in shows and performances, and a desire to impress others. Thus he hides either behind a cloak of invisibility, or behind a role, a performance, a relationship, which has been prepared beforehand. He is unguarded only when his attention is reflexively fixed on some aspect of his own art.

Prospero's farewell to magic is followed by what seems to me to be the strangest and most revealing scene in the play. He assembles the still charmed Europeans in the magic circle, and before they have been allowed to regain their senses, he preaches to them. After some words of praise and promises of reward for Gonzalo, he turns to Alonso and the others:

> Most cruelly
> Didst thou, Alonso, use me and my daughter.
> Thy brother was a furtherer in the act.
> Thou art pinched for 't now, Sebastian. Flesh and blood,
> You, brother mine, that entertained ambition,
> Expelled remorse and nature; who, with Sebastian
> (Whose inward pinches therefore are most strong),
> Would here have killed your king, I do forgive thee,
> Unnatural though thou art.
>
> (5.1.71–79)

No one hears this but Ariel; it is, in effect, a soliloquy. It is as if he hesitates to put on the real scene without one more dress rehearsal; or as if he is primarily aiming the words at himself of the part he has decided to play, and of the parts he has written for them, as penitents. He seems less concerned about Alonso here, and more about Sebastian and Antonio; he has fewer doubts about Alonso, but he has no reason to think that the others have been or could be pinched in any world but the world of his morality play; only when they stand distracted in the magic circle of the microsphere will he trust them to follow his script.

When they return to their senses, a few moments later, his actual playing of the recognition scene is inflected very differently. The final act has little to do with disenchantment, with morality, forgiveness, and contrition. Or at least if these occur they do so only in a play Prospero puts on, and this is something of which he seems quite aware: It is a logical development of his feeling that he cannot in any real sense new-create souls or catch consciences unless the others play the moral parts he has written for them. Therefore, he runs back into magic and art. Of the play's final 214 lines, one sentence is devoted to gently pinching Alonso's conscience, followed later by 32 lines of cat-and-mouse about Ferdinand's supposed death, which has less to do with arousing contrition than with what Clifford

Leech irritatedly calls the "celestial stage-manager at work once again, . . . the almighty contriver [who] must be allowed his thrill in building up his effect." Prospero allows himself four-and-a-half lines to warn Sebastian and Antonio of his power over them, through his knowledge of their conspiracy; five-and-a-half to throw Antonio a cold pardon—really a contemptuous dismissal—and reclaim his dukedom. For the rest, morality, contrition, and forgiveness take a back seat to the miraculous return of the lost prince, the subtleties of the island, and the theatrical *chef d'oeuvre* of the genius at the magic console. In his finest hour, he hogs the stage as actor, director, and hero; as the official greeter welcoming the visitors aboard; as the presenter supplying explanations and promising more entertainment after dinner; as the impresario busily pouring wonders, surprises, and reunions out of his baroque bag of tricks.

This is so clearly his last fling that I find it hard to accept the sentimental interpretation which centers merely on the fact of Prospero's renunciation and return. At the end he seems more unwilling to leave than ever. The closer he gets to leaving, the more Shakespeare shows him protracting and delaying the inevitable conclusion. Four times, beginning with "our revels now are ended," he bids farewell to his art and island, and prepares to leave (4.1.148; 5.1.29, 34, 64). Four times he reminds Ariel that he will soon be free (4.1.261; 5.1.5, 95, 241). On three different occasions he promises to tell his story later (5.1.162, 247, 302), which is a way of attenuating the absoluteness of the break, and extending the experience into the future. Throughout the fifth act his attention is centered on the present enjoyment of his magic and his theatrical triumph. Finally, with the air of one winding things up, he looks forward to his return to Milan; promises good sailing on the morrow, and—at long last—frees Ariel. At this point, the audience begins to think of leaving. But not Prospero: His momentum carries him *through* the end of the play: Before we can flex a muscle or raise hands in applause, before the other characters can have vacated the stage, he has moved toward us; stopped us with "Please you draw near"; and in the tuneless, oddly skewed cadences of the epilogue, has asked us to release him too from "this bare island"—bare of magic, of other characters, of the play itself; a no-man's-land between conclusion and egress; now an apron in the theater more than an island in the sea:

> Now my charms are all o'erthrown,
> And what strength I have 's my own,
> Which is most faint. Now 'tis true
> I must be here confined by you,

Or sent to Naples. Let me not,
Since I have my dukedom got
And pardoned the deceiver, dwell
In this bare island by your spell;
But release me from my bands
With the help of your good hands.
Gentle breath of yours my sails
Must fill, or else my project fails,
Which was to please. Now I want
Spirits to enforce, art to enchant;
And my ending is despair
Unless I be relieved by prayer,
Which pierces so that it assaults
Mercy itself and frees all faults.
As you from crimes would pardoned be,
Let your indulgence set me free.

This is his final and most telling gesture, not only of delay, but also of scene stealing. Yet its mood is in sharp contrast to the theatrical *carpe diem* of the previous scene. The first impression is that of drained energy; literally, of collapsed spirits. And this is of course essential to bring out the true strain of feeling under his exhilaration in the final act; a strain which might otherwise have been visible only in his aside to Miranda's "Brave new world": " 'Tis new to thee." But the epilogue is not easy to make out, because so much of what has happened is packed into it. Voicing his plea in the situational metaphors generated by the play—magic, performance, sailing, and pardon—he asks the help of the spectators' "good hands," first in applause, and then in prayer. The interesting thing about this is that in asking to be freed, asking for auspicious winds and pardon, he places himself in the same relation to the audience as previously Ariel, the Italians, and also Caliban, had stood to him. If we think of him as Ariel, then he is asking to vanish into thin air, or into a cowslip's bell, or wherever he may be far from humanity; for he has, he hopes, done his spriting correspondently, has answered to the spectator's higher and more disengaged pleasures in art. As Caliban, asking to be released from his laborious service, seeking a new master, or simply grace from his present master, as Caliban he asks the audience to pray for him, pardon him, and release him from a bondage which comes to sound more ethical than theatrical toward the end of the epilogue. He may indeed claim to have been a scapegoat for the audience, to have taken their sins upon himself and reflected their true nature or true longings; to have lived their idyllic urges for them and so perhaps, to have helped them stay in the world; to have kept them from his crime, which consisted of asking too much of that world, and giving too little. Finally, he may, as the reinstated Duke of Milan, be begging *them* to help *him* return to the world.

And yet this is not all. The other side of this closing performance is that it is gratuitous; it keeps him from returning to Milan, and from leaving the stage; it momentarily frees him from rounding out his little life, and it allows him to solicit a further range of spectators. He has tried to work on the souls of others; he has at least produced the expected happy ending; and now he moves toward us, as if he is not really at ease about that accomplishment. He wants to be reassured about the success of his project, "which was to please." He continues to play on the spectators as he had on the characters, trying out his new role as mere fellow mortal, testing the audience response, to the end. An indecisive air dominates the tone and rhythm of the epilogue almost to the end; it leaves us wondering whether he is entirely sincere in claiming that his project was to please:

> my ending is despair
> Unless I be relieved by prayer,
> Which pierces so that it assaults
> Mercy itself and frees all faults.
> As you from crimes would pardoned be,
> Let your indulgence set me free.

Here, as throughout the speech, the reference hovers uncertainly between the options of applause and prayer, the plight of the entertainer and of the sinner, the spectator's concern for pleasure and for moral profit. The lines which introduce the request can go both ways: "release me from my bands / With the help of your good hands." And the final line may mean no more than, "be kind to the player and at least indulge him to the extent of *showing* your enjoyment." If we take these words as the utterance of the character and entertainer Prospero, rather than of Burbage or Shakespeare, then we are obliged to reconcile this sense with the other one.

The same words may offer the audience a share in Prospero's mood of weariness, and in his growing conviction that it will take more than human magic to work any changes in our old stock. I think the point of these two very different levels of reference, working together and at cross-purposes in the same set of words, is that Prospero is not sure of his audience. He knows—or suspects—that there are more Trinculos and Antonios than there are Gonzalos and Alonsos among the spectators. He offers them two kinds of response: one for those who may be moved by an appeal to common humanity and sympathy, and who may have received the play and its message at the level of conscience; but another for observers who may be more cynical, or more disillusioned, or merely more casual, and who have for this variety of reasons come to the theater to be entertained, to be briefly transported to another world, to be spellbound by the combined magic and machinery of the spectacle, and to be released new-created at play's end. Yet this is not all. The end is a final attempt to reestablish mastery. The closing couplet has too much bite and sweep to it to be characterized as expressing weariness alone. It points the finger; it does not simply play on the spectator's sympathy; it reminds him of the bond of common humanity which obliges him to assist Prospero. He has shifted his role slightly but significantly in the final couplet, from that of fellow sinner to that of homilist, the voice of conscience. It is part of his refusal to vanish that at the very end, before losing all his strength and art, he *wills,* he ritually bequeathes, his role to the audience. And at the same time this effort at mastery, like those which preceded it during the play, is a dress rehearsal. It is our first view of Prospero in the real world, standing beyond the confines of his magic circle, preparing to confront life with only the ordinary means of persuasion. The epilogue is thus another prologue; he is still tentative and still experimental; still unresolved and still on the verge of a new phase of life. Although he knows his word is less than the miraculous harp, he lays the harp aside.

The Eye of the Storm: Structure and Myth in Shakespeare's *Tempest*

Marjorie Garber

Northrop Frye's *Anatomy of Criticism* begins with what he calls a "Polemical Introduction" (a title most critics must, at one time or another, have envied him). Setting out to expose the ordered patterns which lay beneath—or within—literary texts, he took a moment to explain how he had come to his conclusions. More than twenty years after the *Anatomy* first appeared, the final paragraph of Frye's introduction stands as both an encouragement and a warning to the critic who would apply taxonomies to literature: "The schematic nature of this book," he wrote, "is deliberate, and is a feature of it that I am unable, after long reflection, to apologize for. There is a place for classification in criticism, as in any other discipline which is more important than an elegant accomplishment of some mandarin caste. The strong emotional repugnance felt by many critics toward any form of schematization in poetics is again the result of a failure to distinguish criticism as a body of knowledge from the direct experience of literature, where every act is unique, and classification has no place. Whenever schematization appears in the following pages, no importance is attached to the schematic form itself, which may be only the result of my own lack of ingenuity. Much of it, I expect, and in fact hope, may be mere scaffolding, to be knocked away when the building is in better shape. The rest of it belongs to the systematic study of the formal causes of art."

It is hard to remember that Frye's "modes," "symbols," "myths," and "genres" were so controversial as to require a polemical defense. But equally

From *The Hebrew University Studies in Literature* 8, no. 1 (Spring 1980). © 1980 by HSL, The Hebrew University, Jerusalem.

striking in this passage is Frye's respect for the humanistic primacy of the critical discipline. The building he constructs—his interpretation of the text—will stand after the scaffolding has been dismantled, but it could not have been built without the scaffolding structure. Following out the metaphor, we may perhaps say that the critic is engaged in a task of *edification,* of which a taxonomic framework is an essential—though temporarily unsightly—part.

The "strong emotional repugnance" toward schematization noted by Frye in 1957 has been even more evident in responses to contemporary critical theory. The word "structuralism," in particular, has alienated a significant number of readers and critics who see the term—borrowed by linguists from anthropology, and by literary critics from linguistics—as announcing a misleadingly "scientific" (or pseudoscientific) approach to literature, far removed from the richly diverse and allusive heritage of humanism. Quite understandably, such skeptics find terms like "binary opposition," "code," "synchronic and diachronic studies," "paradigmatic and syntagmatic relations" uncomfortably close to a language of mechanical, computer-like precision which threatens to reduce poetry to numbers and signs. Moreover, those who persevere beyond the terminology to consider the practical results of structuralist analysis are often moved to suggest that the Emperor has no clothes: that after a tortuous application of his privileged language and methods, the structuralist critic does not produce insights markedly different from those of more traditional thematic critics, myth critics, formalists, and the like. On the other hand, those who find the structuralist approach interesting and valuable are often moved to make unrealistic claims for the uniqueness of their work, so that the reader is offered an awkward choice: structuralism as a pretentious redundancy, or structuralism as the pioneering truth.

In fact, structuralist literary criticism is neither the heresy nor the revealed truth it is sometimes thought to be. Rather, it is another way of looking at the details of a literary work, and putting them together in a persuasive, illuminating way. In other words, properly used it is a kind of close reading, which focuses the reader's attention upon significant comparisons, contrasts, and patterns which more impressionistic methods sometimes neglect, in a way that places a strong emphasis upon the process of reading itself.

Two examples chosen from the wealth of contemporary criticism on *The Tempest* may help to make this point clear. In his recent book, *The Heart's Forest,* David Young argues that the play is a version of pastoral, and explores its patterns of paradox and antithesis, observing that "confinement and freedom, mastery and servitude, are not so much unalterable opposites as they are mutually complementary aspects of the same thing." Young is principally interested in the larger thematic antitheses which in his view animate the pastorals—Nature and Art, Nature and Nurture, Nature and Fortune—but his study felicitously approaches the entire question of opposites which delimit and therefore define. He does not call them binary oppositions, but in a sense that is what they are: functional contrasts which demarcate classes, and provide a basis for further analysis. Thus Young, certainly not a structuralist, makes productive use of a technique which structuralism has claimed as peculiarly its own.

On the other end of the scale we might consider a recent essay by Jan Kott, whose title, "*The Tempest,* or Repetition," suggests the nature of his concern. Kott contends that the play is built upon the "significant and characteristic confrontation between two linguistic codes—of historical experience and of the Virgilean myth." The plantations of the New World and the golden age of Greek and Roman myth are both "repeated" in Prospero's experience on the island, but the repetition is not a purgation. According to Kott, Prospero "knew that the future was to bring merely another repetition" when he left for his exile, and during the course of the play "everything is repeated . . . but nothing purified." Hence he argues that *The Tempest* is "the most bitter of Shakespeare's plays," "the lost hopes of the Renaissance." Kott's article makes extensive use of the language of structuralism, identifying not only repetitions but also binary oppositions, codes and signs, and his text makes thorny reading for one unfamiliar with the special use structuralism has come to make of these terms. But the conclusions he draws are based less upon his method of structural analysis than upon his conviction that the play is a "bitter" one. "Shakespeare had no illusions," he tells us. Like Young—and like the present writer—Kott comments on the dialectic between confinement and release; so indeed have many critics, since the pattern is readily discerned in the play. But whereas Young suggests that "confinement, rightly borne, can lead to freedom," Kott sees the play's concept of freedom as "sardonic," and finds in Caliban's freedom song a "repetition" of Brutus's cry, "Peace, freedom, and liberty!" on the assassination of Julius Caesar. In short, Kott offers an argument congenial to structuralist (as well as much post-structuralist and nihilist) criticism, but hardly the only one possible from the identification of contrasts and repetitions in the play—as my own very different conclusions will try to show.

Like other critical methods, structuralism is most enlightening when used with judgment and restraint. Literary orthodoxies easily become parodic versions of themselves, and an orthodoxy with a built-in jargon is more than usually susceptible to such a fate. Nonetheless, even for those of us who do not think of ourselves as structuralists, the techniques developed by these critics can offer much that is valuable in augmenting more traditional ways of reading. Structuralist categories like "binarism" and "deep structure" can lead the reader to see patterns heretofore unsuspected and, equally important, to recognize important relations among those patterns. Such relations provide a "scaffolding" analogous to Frye's, from which a persuasive interpretation can be built. *The Tempest,* with its distinctive network of interwoven events, seems particularly well-suited to such an approach. Further, structuralism places its emphasis upon the experiences of the *reader*—or by extension, in the case of a dramatic work, the *audience.* Jonathan Culler, in his lucid and helpful study *Structuralist Poetics,* puts the general case well: "Though [structuralism] does not, of course, replace ordinary thematic interpretation, it does avoid premature foreclosure—the unseemly rush from word to world—and stays within the literary system for as long as possible. Insisting that literature is something other than a statement about the world, it establishes, finally, an analogy between the production or reading of signs in literature and in other areas of experience and studies the ways in which the former explores and dramatizes the limitations of the latter. In this kind of interpretation the meaning of the work is what it shows the reader, by the acrobatics in which it involves him, about the problems of his condition as *homo significans,* maker and reader of signs." By substituting *audience* for *reader* here, we may observe once again that *The Tempest,* with its concentric series of audiences (mariners, Neapolitans, Miranda and Ferdinand, the audience in the theater) is an especially fit subject for a scrutiny that draws in part upon structuralist techniques. The play poses a number of provocative perceptual questions for its audience, inviting us to speculate about the singular way in which we understand—and respond to—its design.

With the single exception of *Love's Labor's Lost,* a very early play, *The Tempest* is the only one of Shakespeare's works for which no source has been found. In this respect, as in so many others, the play presents its audience with something rich and strange. Creatures like Ariel and Caliban appear nowhere else in Shakespeare, nor in the works of his contemporary dramatists; next to them even the fairies of *A Midsummer Night's Dream* appear almost commonplace. Nowhere else do we find a figure quite like Prospero, compelling and almost omniscient, and his island, with its several strange shapes and thousand twangling instruments, is like no other magic world in literature, history, or art. Yet for all the strangeness of these

inventions, we find them, I think, immediately persuasive. For most audiences the experience of *The Tempest* is oddly but persistently one of
recognition, of remembering; rather like the bemused mariners of act 5,
we seem to have slept and dreamed this all before. How can we account
for this curious feeling of familiarity and recognition, a feeling, not that
we are encountering the merely bizarre, but rather that we are reacquainting
ourselves with something we have long known or believed? How does
Shakespeare achieve this feat of dramatic legerdemain, transforming his last
great play virtually into a retrospective source for the rest of his art? The
answers, if there are answers, may well lie in the kindred realms of structure
and myth in *The Tempest*; to seek them out, we should begin with the
"shape invisible" which is the play.

One way of approaching the design of *The Tempest* is to consider it
as founded upon a series of parallel lines, each of which constitutes both
an axis and a spectrum. One such line could be described as macrocosmic,
spanning the four elements so as to transform Shakespeare's Globe into a
replica of the physical globe. Caliban is a spirit of earth and water, Ariel a
spirit of fire and air, and together they are harnessed by Prospero to perform
all actions necessary to man. A second spectrum could be identified as
microcosmic, its structural shape not that of the exterior universe, but rather
the interior of a man's mind. Here Caliban signifies the libido and the id.
He lusts after Miranda, and would have raped her and peopled the isle with
Calibans, but, at the same time, as Prospero says, "We cannot miss him,"
since "he does make our fire, / Fetch in our wood, and serves in offices /
That profit us" (1.2.313–15). Caliban exemplifies the dark but necessary
part of every man: this thing of darkness I acknowledge mine. At the other
end of this spectrum, of course, stands Ariel once more, this time as the
embodiment of the imagination, the spirit of music, art, and the fleeting
capacities of genius, which can be captured briefly, but must always be let
go. Again Prospero delimits and animates the spectrum; it is, in a sense,
his mind that we see expanded and mirrored upon the stage.

A third line upon the imaginary graph we are constructing would
indicate one of the basic precepts of Renaissance philosophy, once more
using Ariel and Caliban as the axial poles of spirit and beast. Here man is
a creature a little lower than the angels, caught between the bestial and the
celestial, a creature of almost infinite possibilities, necessarily mindful of
both his superiority and his limitations. If we liked, we could vary our
terminology, and call these parallel lines by such names as physical reality,
psychology, and philosophy, without altering their basically synchronous
relation; in fact, such labelling merely serves to underscore the fact that that

play is operating within several different systems of signification, to generate a unified fable. We could even go further, and adduce a number of additional spectra or axes, for example, a spectrum of language, which would extend from the "excellent dumb discourse" of the several strange shapes, and the voice of Ariel as wind spirit or Harpy, through Ferdinand's astonishment that Miranda speaks "my language? Heavens!" (1.2.431) (or, as Stephano less delicately says of Caliban, "Where the devil should he learn our language?" [2.2.66–67]), all the way to Caliban's own "You taught me language, and my profit on't / Is, I know how to curse" (1.2.365–66). The fundamental elements of the spectrum in this case would be (1) a magic spiritual language unavailable to human beings; (2) Italian, a language of human interchange; and (3) cursing, utterance without communicative value. Similarly, a scale we could label "anthropological" would extend from the amphibious Caliban, whose name recalls Montaigne's "Of Cannibals," to the evanescent and occasionally bodiless Ariel, with the humans ranged on a continuum between them, starting at the low end with Trinculo, and extending as far up as Prospero or Miranda. What all of this may serve to demonstrate is not only the multiplicity of interpretative systems on which the play is constructed, but also a factor common to all the spectra we have described. Each is in fact roughly tripartite, the extreme poles signifying aspects of subhuman or superhuman behavior, the middle portion occupied by varieties of human activity. We could draw three vertical lines down our almost infinite series of parallels, and in so doing form a grid, the common horizontal coordinates of which would be beast, man, and god.

We are now prepared to collapse these tripartite or continuous formulations into binary oppositions, and in so doing to reduce the continuous to the discrete—a necessary first step in the process of interpretation, since it provides us with distinct and therefore analyzable classes. The first method which suggests itself here—and on the face of things a perfectly acceptable one—is the simple subtraction of the central term, yielding such oppositions as god/beast, song/curse, fire/water, and freedom/bondage. All of these, as we shall see, are essential to the design of *The Tempest*. But to withdraw the central term, the human component, is both limiting and artificial. Shakespeare's play does not do this, and in fact it might be argued that no play, certainly no Shakespearean play, could do so. Drama, after all, is the literary genre which comes closest to fulfilling the structuralist ideal of disappearance of the self; for the self, the lyric or narrative voice, it substitutes the audience.

Nowhere, perhaps, is this more clear than in the second scene of *The*

Tempest, in which the audience in the theater joins with Miranda, the audience on the stage, in suffering at the sight of the shipwreck and the storm. Gradually Prospero unfolds the true state of affairs to his daughter, and just as gradually we in the audience are enlightened, and brought to realize that what we have interpreted as storm and chaos is actually a function of order and art. The tempest itself is a sign, which we must be taught to decode or interpret correctly.

As Miranda watches the shipwreck, and we watch with her, the human perspective intrudes itself upon the magical phenomena. Miranda is the ideal audience of tragedy, caught up in a catharsis of pity and fear, suffering with those that she saw suffer. That the play turns out to have a happy ending is in part a result of her vicarious participation in the tragic experience to which she is a witness—and in part, too, a result of the same participation on the part of the audience. The often criticized epilogue to the play reinforces this crucial truth: the audience, explicitly *as* audience, by clapping and cheering with "good hands" and "gentle breath," is called upon to liberate Prospero from the island, and the human actor from his role. His art abandoned, his charms o'erthrown, Prospero stands at the last as an emblem of the merely yet transcendently human: the Duke of Milan mindful of the grave, and the actor conscious of the mutability of all roles.

In selecting among the possible sets of binary oppositions generated by the play, then, we may be prepared to discover that while the god/beast is a valuable and accurate nexus of classification, it can be greatly improved by being split into two constituent parts, god/man and beast/man. This is clearly borne out in the design of the play, in which the immediate perception of a binary opposition between Caliban and Ariel gives place, before long, to a more dramatically energized binarism between Caliban and Ferdinand. Both, for example, are sons of hereditary rulers, who view themselves as heirs to power; both are suitors to Miranda; and, most importantly, both participate in a central pattern which, as we shall see, can most easily be described in terms of the binarism freedom/bondage. Similarly, there is a useful comparison to be made between Caliban and Miranda, both nurtured on the island, both pupils of Prospero, but radically opposed, of course, on the axis of nature and nurture, or original sin and grace.

By following this procedure, we can discover a series of genuinely enlightening oppositions. For example, the axis which extends from Sycorax's black magic, to human absence of magic, to Prospero's white, theurgic magic, can be readily converted to the binary opposition art/humanity which we discerned in the second scene. The binarism freedom/bondage, representing a god/beast polarity, might be said as well to contain a hidden medial term which could be designated as "government," or "law." On the other hand, another way of describing the same freedom/ bondage polarity would be to translate it, in the play's terms, into the fraternal or filial relation, usurpation/obedience. In this case the transformation reveals an implicit inversion: freedom can be bestial, bondage ameliorative. In point of fact, the dialectic of freedom and bondage in the play emphasizes just such a transformation. Ferdinand, apparently freed by the shipwreck even of filial bonds, at once elects another sort of bondage when he sees Miranda:

> My spirits, as in a dream, are all bound up.
> My father's loss, the weakness which I feel,
> The wrack of all my friends, not this man's threats
> To whom I am subjued, are but light to me,
> Might I but through my prison once a day
> Behold this maid. All corners else o' th'earth
> Let liberty make use of. Space enough
> Have I in such a prison.
>
> (1.2.490–97)

Literally spellbound by Prospero's charm, which keeps him from moving, Ferdinand cherishes his bondage. By contrast Caliban is freed, although by liquor rather than by love. His error is the same as that outlined in Gonzalo's portrait of the ideal commonwealth, the supposition that post-lapsarian man is innocent and therefore may justly have "no occupation; all men idle, all . . . No sovereignty" (2.1.159–61). Carolling his anthem of liberation,

> 'Ban, 'Ban, Ca-Caliban
> Has a new master. Get a new man!
> Freedom, high day! High day, freedom! Freedom,
> high day, freedom!
>
> (2.2.186–89)

Caliban lurches off toward his fate, his words here as ominous as the burden of his later song, "Thought is free." As if to emphasize the element of binary opposition here, this scene, which closes act 2, is immediately juxtaposed to the opening stage direction of act 3, "Enter Ferdinand, bearing a log." Ferdinand, of course, is the new man Prospero has gotten, speaking the language of bondage or "service": "The mistress which I serve quickens what's dead/And makes my labors pleasures" (3.1.6–7); and, "The very instant that I saw you, did/My heart fly to your service" (ll. 64–65).

Interestingly, Prospero will later make this same argument to Ariel, emphasizing that freedom is in truth a factor of bondage:

> Shortly shall all my labors end, and thou
> Shalt have the air at freedom. For a little,
> Follow, and do me service.
>
> (4.1.264–66)

The image of Ferdinand as Prospero's "new man" should also call to mind Saint Paul's injunction to the Ephesians, to put off the old man and put on the new man (Eph. 4:22–24). In this case, the juxtaposition of scenes, from Caliban in 2.2 to Ferdinand in 3.1, clearly accentuates the structural opposition between the two characters. We might hypothesize, then, that the very dynamic of the play's construction is binary.

In support of such a contention, we may point to a number of further correspondences in *The Tempest*. There are two sets of conspirators, high and low, courtiers and servants. In a pair of parallel scenes, both sets are tempted, in ways which are suggestively reminiscent of the temptation of Tantalos, another kingly figure who sought to arrogate power not appropriately his. Tantalos decided to test the gods in order to prove his superiority to them; in punishment, he was condemned to stand forever in a pool of water, reaching for fruit which hung above his head. As he bent to drink, the waters receded, and as he reached to pluck the fruit, the boughs lifted out of reach. Likewise, in 3.3, Ariel tempts the court party with a spectral banquet, but as the usurping nobles, Antonio, Sebastian, and Alonso, reach out to "feed" upon the banquet, it disappears "with a quaint device," and leaves Ariel as a Harpy to confront the "three men of sin." Shortly thereafter, in 4.1, we witness the parallel discomfiture of the mock-court ruled by Stephano. Reaching for "glistering apparel" which Caliban alone recognizes as trash, they are left by Ariel "I' th' filthy mantled pool beyond [Prospero's] cell" (4.1.182).

Let us consider one further evidence of scene juxtaposition, to verify the prevalence of such devices in the play, and measure their significance for the dynamics of both meaning and action. In act 2, scene 1, we hear Alonso mourning for the supposed death of his son Ferdinand:

> O thou mine heir
> Of Naples and of Milan, what strange fish
> Hath made his meal on thee?
>
> (ll. 116–18)

An Elizabethan audience, hearing this lament, might well call to mind a relevant biblical passage from the Book of Jonah: "Now the Lord had prepared a great fish to swallow up Jonah. And Jonah was in the belly of the fish three days and three nights" (1:17–18). Unsurprisingly, the Renaissance understood this passage to suggest that Jonah was a type of Christ, and since Ferdinand associates himself explicitly with resurrection ("a second life"), the two figures are for a moment twinned.

In the next scene, however, the strange fish comes to life, and reveals itself as Caliban. "What have we here? A man or a fish? . . . A fish!" (2.2.24–26), comments Trinculo, creeping under Caliban's garment to protect himself from thunder. To the audience in the theater, what is now visible is the image of four arms and four legs extending from under a tarpaulin—a spectacle which Stephano interprets as "some monster of the isle." Caliban has, in effect, swallowed up Trinculo. But which is the real monster, the half-man, half-beast? Literally, of course, it is Caliban; Trinculo calls him a "perfidious and drunken monster." And yet upon consideration it is clear that all of these terms apply even more appropriately to Trinculo himself. Endowed with the capacity for fully human conduct, ostensibly civilized and educated, he exhibits nonetheless the full catalogue of monstrous characteristics. What we have here, in short, is a visual conflation which yields a persuasive metaphor. Figurative monster is conflated with literal monster, and the upward metamorphosis from man to god in the Jonah story is juxtaposed to the downward metamorphosis of man to beast in the sorry adventures of Trinculo.

Nor is this the end of the chain of correspondences, for the following scene presents the interview between Ferdinand and Miranda, in which he first learns her name. In their previous encounter, lacking this information, he had intuitively addressed her as "O you wonder!" (1.2.429). Now he exclaims, "Admired Miranda!" (3.1.37)—or, as we might translate, "wonderful wonder; admired admired one." Trinculo has been transformed onstage from figurative to literal monster and now Miranda, a figurative wonder, has revealed herself to bear the very name of her condition.

We are now, perhaps, in a position to see more clearly why The Tempest evokes in its audience a feeling so much akin to recognition, why our acceptance of the fable it has to tell is so complete, and why its events and actions, though they have no known source, appear to be so familiar. For one thing, the play is constructed along parallel axes in such a way that its themes, subjects, and contexts can all be translated into systems with the coordinates god/man/beast. It thus possesses an inherent and pervasive unity far beyond the neoclassical unities of time, place, and action. We are, in effect, seeing the same story told over and over again, simultaneously— or, to put it in other terms, the action of the play is at the same time synchronic and diachronic. The principal dramatic action takes place in the present, encompassing the period from the shipwreck to Prospero's epilogue, or from the beginning of act 1 to the end of act 5. Its method is synchronic, describing the system of the play as a functional whole: the relationship of one character to another, and one scene to the next. But other aspects of the action—like the fact that this is a *second* shipwreck, and a *second* attempt at usurpation—indicate the presence of a diachronic pattern, which describes the historical development of the play's events over time. Moreover, the play's technique or methodology is one of repetition and juxtaposition. Caliban is juxtaposed to Ariel, to Ferdinand, and to Miranda; a body of "high" conspirators is succeeded by a body of "low" conspirators, both bent on usurpation; a scene of self-delusive "freedom" is placed next to a scene of willing and beneficent bondage. Such juxtapositions or binary oppositions pinpoint crucial areas of meaning, by indicating the thematic axes of which they form a part; thus freedom/bondage, for example, suggests the existence of a continuum concerned with the subjects of law, desire, and rule. In short, the principles of parallelism and binarism, essential to the structuralist analysis of any system, are present in the formal stucture of *The Tempest* to an extreme degree. This orderliness, or congruence, suggests both a layering and a concentration of meaning, just as the tempest with which the play begins differs from, and yet recapitulates, the tempest twelve years earlier, which brought Prospero and Miranda to the refuge of the island. The play is in effect a palimpsest, on which each succeeding system writes, in its own language, the same message.

Yet this explanation, while persuasive to a degree, does not fully answer the question with which we began. There remains the necessity to investigate the deep structure of *The Tempest,* to isolate and scrutinize the elements which constitute its basic fable. And if we attempt to do this, we discover a most interesting pattern. We discover that the play is about a human artist-magician whose time is divided between the locking up of monster-men (Caliban, the high and low conspirators), and the freeing of godlike men (Ferdinand, Miranda, Prospero himself, even by license Ariel). The degree of success and failure he brings to these two tasks determines the possibility of his own escape, and is related to his acknowledgement of his own humanity and mortality. Whether Shakespeare was aware, when he wrote *The Tempest,* of any correspondence this pattern may have had with previous literature or myth, it is neither possible nor necessary to say. But it is reasonable to speculate that a Renaissance reader, and particularly a Renaissance mythographer, might have seen a faint light cast by these figures into the dark backward and abysm of time. For the pattern of

Prospero, poised between Ariel and Caliban, is also the pattern of the greatest artisan in all of Greek mythology—the pattern of Daedalus.

The Renaissance considered Daedalus principally as an artist and scientist, the chief ancient practitioner of the "Mechanicall artes." Ben Jonson, who gave Daedalus a place of honor in his masque *Pleasure Reconciled to Virtue*, pictures him there as an archtypal artisan, leading a series of maze-like dances commemorating wisdom, beauty, and love: "All actions of mankind," says his chant, "are but a labyrinth or maze" (ll. 232–33). Renaissance mythographers saw the story of Daedalus as indicative of both the power and the hubris of the artist: "for Mechanicall artes are of ambiguous use, serving as well for hurt as for remedy, and they have in a manner power both to loose and bind themselves." At the same time, somewhat whimsically from a modern viewpoint, Daedalus was considered a figure of parental authority, and we hear that "Icarus is justly punished for refusing to hearken to his father's counsell, a good lesson for all children." As these excerpts will show, there were in a sense two Daedaluses, or at least two stories about Daedalus: Daedalus and Icarus, and Daedalus, builder of the labyrinth. If we look at this pair of stories more closely, however, we will perceive that they are really aspects of the same story, in which the artist, who exemplifies the best of mankind, attempts to define himself against the sub- and the super-human. He constructs the labyrinth and thus by his art confines and controls the Minotaur; he constructs, as well, the waxen wings, enabling his son and himself to escape and to aspire toward the heavens—but Icarus, failing to perceive the necessary difference between himself and the gods, flies too close to the sun and falls to his death. In both cases, the efforts of Daedalus could be described as pursuing exactly the model of binary opposition we have just considered: by confronting what he is not, man delimits and declares what he is.

In measuring the Daedalus story against the story of *The Tempest*, it will be helpful to deal with the two episodes discretely. The story of Daedalus and Icarus is in essence a fable of failed education. The father is unable to persuade his son of the urgency of his advice; hence the rather comic Renaissance feeling that the story is preeminently one of filial disobedience. But this theme of filial disobedience is in fact a central one for the play, as it is throughout Shakespeare's romances. From the opening episode of the storm we see and hear Prospero continually cautioning Miranda to "attend me," "Mark me." His pretense of sternness with Ferdinand is a potential father's test, and his obsession with chastity is part of the structure of necessary law which we saw earlier suggested by the matter of attribution of godhead. Icarus fails, and falls, because he refuses to accept a distinction between himself and the gods; like the humble human spectators of Ovid's account, he "credidit esse deos" (*Metamorphoses*), he thought they must be gods. The same temptation comes to Miranda, and to Ferdinand; each, meeting the other for the first time, expresses a like conviction:

> MIRANDA: I might call him
> A thing divine; for nothing natural
> I ever saw so noble
>
> .   .   .   .
>
> FERDINAND: Most sure, the goddess
> On whom these airs attend!
>
> (1.2.420–22; 424–25)

Prospero's response to those declarations is immediate and decided; it is, in fact, one of the intemperances about Prospero's persona which this line of inquiry may help to justify.

> MIRANDA: It carries a brave form. But 'tis a spirit.
> PROSPERO: No, wench; it eats, and sleeps, and hath such senses
> As we have, such.
>
> (ll. 414–16)

The series of events that follows, in which Ferdinand confirms his humanity by carrying logs, is once more interrupted at the time of the fertility pageant, where Ferdinand's unconsidered cry, "Let me live here ever!" (4.1.122), leads directly to the dissolution of the masque and a renewed awareness of the threat to Prospero's life. Education, in the sense in which Prospero offers it to Miranda, will prove to be a literal leading out—out of childhood, and out of the protected venue of the island. Prospero's deep and abiding concern to emphasize Ferdinand's mortality, and thereby Miranda's, is a direct controversion of the Icarus model. Daedalus fails to persuade Icarus of his limitations, and he dies; Prospero succeeds in persuading Miranda of Ferdinand's (and her own), and Miranda and Ferdinand escape the island to become King and Queen of Naples. It is this controversion which constitutes a new kind of binary opposition: acceptance/rejection of human identity.

To underscore the importance of the distinction between man and god upon the island, Shakespeare provides us with a parodic example. As Ferdinand's first contact with the island's inhabitants leads him to suppose them gods, so a first meeting with Stephano has the same effect upon Caliban. Carrying the bottle which is his counterpart of Prospero's magic books, Stephano reels onto the stage, and pours a drink for Caliban.

> CALIBAN: [Aside.] These be fine things, and if they be not
> sprites.
> That's a brave god and bears celestial liquor.
> I will kneel to him
>
> . . . .
>
> I'll swear upon that bottle to be thy true
> subject, for the liquor is not earthly
>
> . . . .
>
> STEPHANO: Here, kiss the book. [*Gives him drink.*]
> (1.2.117–19; 125–26; 130)

Caliban, throughout the play compared with Ferdinand, here makes an error which is at once ludicrous and dangerous; taking a man for his god, he finds himself, as a result, driven by spirits in the shapes of dogs and hounds, and plagued with "dry convulsions" and "aged cramps"—the physical debilities of old age. His "celestial" attempt at usurpation—ascension to Prospero's place of godhead—results in a brush with hell and death.

In a way, however, the dangers of thinking oneself a god—or one's beloved a goddess—are less perilous to Ferdinand and Miranda than they are to Prospero himself. For Prospero is very like a god. From the inception of the play we see that by his art he can, like a wrathful Jehovah, raise a flood to destroy the wicked. Miranda, pleading with him to halt the storm, expresses the analogy in a conditional phrase: "Had I been any god of power, I would/Have sunk the sea within the earth or ere/It should the good ship to have swallowed" (1.2.10–12). Prospero *is* a god of power in the context of the island; he commands sprites, keeps Ariel and Caliban under his direction, even penetrates, through Ariel's skill, into the malevolent imaginations of his enemies. In such a situation Daedalus is in danger of becoming Icarus, as the Renaissance mythographers seem almost to have anticipated: "Let us take heed of curiosity, pry not too much into the secrets of God," writes one, "lest we have *Icarus* his reward: for all humane reason is but waxen wings." And again, "Astronomers, and such as undertake to foretell future contingencies, or will take upon them such things as pass human power, are like *Icarus*; they fall at last into a sea of contempt and scorn."

Prospero's susceptibility to such vanities of power is established from the outset; his present exile results directly from his raptness in "secret studies" and his consequent neglect of civil governance. Once upon the island, he does not, like Daedalus and Icarus, attempt literal flight; that characteristic is displaced to the figure of Ariel, who embodies many of the mythological attributes of power—without the power. But "flight" as a thematic nexus is crucial to the play, nonetheless, for it points to a binarism which is at the center of Prospero's dilemma. Ariel has "flight," the art of winged ascent; he lacks, however, the power of another kind of "flight," escape. In fact it is his very possession of such attributes as godlike flight which makes Prospero so anxious to retain him. As for Prospero, his godlike qualities, too, threaten to delay his escape. For a moment his wrath at the conspirators appears unbounded, and in place of a harmonious return to Milan and mortality, "where/Every third thought shall be my grave" (5.1.311–12), we see an autocrat of the imagination, eager to exact his vengeance. At the beginning of act 5 Prospero appears in his magic robes with Ariel at his side, and even the time of day serves to emphasize his Elohistic role.

> PROSPERO: How's the day?
> ARIEL: On the sixth hour, at which time, my lord,
>   You said our work should cease.
>
>   (5.1.3–5)

But neither on the sixth hour, nor on the sixth day, will the power of Prospero cease, until he too is educated, led out of vengeance toward "the rarer action," virtue—out of the Old Testament into the New. Significantly, it is Ariel, possessed of flight and the physical attributes of godhead, who persuades Prospero back toward his own humanity, in one of the most moving scenes in all of Shakespeare:

> ARIEL: Your charm so strongly works 'em,
>   That if you now beheld them, your affections
>   Would become tender.
> PROSPERO: Dost thou think so, spirit?
> ARIEL: Mine would, sir, were I human.
> PROSPERO: And mine shall.
>   Hast thou, which art but air, a touch, a feeling
>   Of their afflictions, and shall not myself
>   One of their kind, that relish all as sharply,
>   Passion as they, be kindlier moved than thou art?
>
>   (5.1.17–24)

At the close of this climactic scene, having given orders for the release of his captives, Prospero delivers his soliloquy of abdication:

> But this rough magic
> I here abjure
>
> . . . . . .
> I'll break my staff,
> Bury it certain fathoms in the earth,
> And deeper than did ever plummet sound
> I'll drown my book.
>
> (ll. 50–57)

This final declaration, "I'll drown my book," speaks directly to the issue of godhead and humanity. Prospero's books are the source of his power, as even Caliban has realized: "Remember / First," he counsels his confederates, "to possess his books; for without them / He's but a sot, as I am" (3.2.94–96). The drowning of the book is thus a straightforward emblem of the abdication of godlike power. But the choice of "drowning" as the mode of renunciation—as opposed, for example, to the more usual "burning" of dangerous books—suggests, as well, a pair of significant correspondences. The play began with a shipwreck and the supposition that all the ship's passengers had perished—by drowning. In the first scene Gonzalo and Antonio are convinced that they will drown. Ferdinand, finding himself safe, speaks with certainty of "my drowned father" (1.2.408), and the term appears some twenty times within the play, always with the same assumption: "Art thou not drowned, Stephano?" (2.2.110); "He is drowned / Whom thus we stray to find" (3.3.8–9). Even tongues are said to drown (in sack), and Caliban, disenchanted by the drunken Stephano, grumbles in exasperation, "The dropsy drown this fool!" (4.1.230). And yet, of all the characters in the play threatened with drowning, literal or metaphorical, not one actually drowns or comes to harm. The *book* is drowned instead of the sinners; grace and human sympathy replace, and displace, superhuman vengeance.

By contrast we may wish to notice that the parties of the Daedalus myth were not so fortunate. Icarus does drown, catapulted from the heights of heaven when his man-made wings begin to melt. Daedalus, the artisan father, has made his son sufficient to have stood—or flown—but free to fall. What are described in Ovid as his "damnosas . . . artes," his fatal arts, have led inexorably to Icarus's death, despite the summary attempts at education. Now the bereaved father "devovit . . . suas artes," cursed his talents, and buried his hapless child. In *The Tempest* the opposite choice is made. The artisan father succeeds in his project of education, and the art is drowned, instead of the child. "I'll drown my book." Ariel, the literal embodiment of the power of flight, is kept in servitude throughout the play and only exults in his freedom to fly when Prospero relinquishes his sorcerer's role. In this way the Icarus story, which the Renaissance interpreted as an injunction to the middle way, functions as a submerged but powerful deep structure, unifying and extending the play's central concern with the necessary distinction between man and god.

But the Icarus story, as we have already noted, is only half of the myth of Daedalus. The other half, the story of the Minotaur, emphasizes with equal directness the necessity of distinguishing between man and beast. The details of the story are well known: Daedalus had assisted Minos's queen, Pasiphae, in satisfying her lust for a great bull, by contriving a wooden cow inside which she crouched to receive his favors. The result of this union was the Minotaur, a monster half-man, half-bull. In order to restrain the malevolence of this monster, which fed on young virgins, Minos instructed Daedalus to build the labyrinth, an impenetrable maze with the Minotaur confined at its center. Later Ariadne would assist the hero Theseus in escaping from the labyrinth after he had slain the Minotaur, by giving him a thread to take with him on his journey toward the center; by following the thread, he was able to negotiate the return journey in safety.

Now, there is clearly much in this story which brings to mind episodes within *The Tempest*. A half-man, half-beast who preys on virgins may well be merely a metaphorical description of any wicked seducer—but it is also a strikingly apt description of Caliban. It is, in fact, in retaliation for his sexual attack upon Miranda that Prospero has confined him:

> For I am all the subjects that you have,
> Which first was mine own king; and here you sty me
> In this hard rock, whiles you do keep from me
> The rest o' th'island.
>
> (1.2.343–46)

I should like to argue that the stying of Caliban in the rock is a gesture within the play precisely analogous to the penning of the Minotaur in the labyrinth. Civilization, in Renaissance terms and in Shakespeare's, could in this context be defined as the art of enclosing the monster within the maze. In both the Daedalus myth and *The Tempest*, it is notable that the encloser is an artist.

Moreover, the literal or visible identity of Caliban with the categories "monster" and "Minotaur" presents only the first of a series of graded equivalents, a sliding scale, so to speak, of monstrosity. We have already seen that Trinculo's characteristics are conflated with those of Caliban (2.2),

and that the parallel treatment of the "high" and "low" conspirators further
develops a sense of kinship among them. Interestingly, the word "monster"
itself, which appears thirty-eight times in the play, is always applied to
Caliban, but "monstrous," which makes a simile of the noun, is appro-
priated by Alonso to describe his own consciousness of guilt:

> O, it is monstrous, monstrous!
> Methought the billows spoke and told me of it;
> The winds did sing it to me; and the thunder,
> That deep and dreadful organ pipe, pronounced
> The name of Prosper; it did bass my trespass.
>   (3.3.95–99)

Clearly the monstrosity here is not confined to Ariel's phenomena of
wind and water; it is the deed, "my trespass," which calls forth this degree
of emotion. Likewise Antonio and Sebastian are more truly monsters than
the creature Caliban, as the artless Gonzalo suggests in his account of the
"several strange shapes":

> though they are of monstrous shape, yet note,
> Their manners are more gentle, kind, than of
> Our human generation you shall find
> Many—nay, almost any.
>   (3.3.31–34)

We hardly need Prospero's instructive aside, ("Honest lord, / Thou
has said well; for some of you there present / Are worse than devils") to
understand the ironic truth of Gonzalo's observation. The presence of a
"real" or literal monster in the play acts as a scale figure, allowing us more
readily to identify and categorize bestiality in human beings. Caliban lusts
for Miranda, the conspirators lust for power; both seek to kill Prospero.
The attempted rape of Miranda and the exile of the innocent and unworldly
Prospero of twelve years past are alike attacks upon virgins, who require,
though they may not desire, the protective education of experience.

The stying of Caliban in the rock is, then, an action strongly parallel
to the enclosure of the Minotaur. In both cases the artist uses his skill to
restrain a subhuman creature, since he cannot destroy him—or, if we consider the same action on the axis of psychology, to repress his own antisocial
impulses by means of socialization and civilization. The trope is not alto-
gether a new one for the Renaissance: Marlowe's plays, for example, are
full of power-wielding monsters enclosed in cages, cauldrons, and dun-
geons. But perhaps the closest iconographic analogue in Renaissance lit-

erature is Spenser's Garden of Adonis, in which the "wilde Bore" which once "annoyd" Adonis is confined by Venus in "a strong rocky Caue" beneath the Mount. While foregoing any speculation about the significance which a boar imprisoned beneath the mount of Venus has for Spenser's view of Platonic love, we may nonetheless firmly recognize this as an activity kindred to Daedalus's—and Prospero's. Clearly the "Bore" is part of the conditions of the garden; Venus does not and presumably cannot kill him, but she can and does "emprison" him "for ay *Faerie Queene*."

Nor do we have to look far to come upon other allusions to the labyrinth and its function, for twice in the course of the play the mystifying circumstances of the plot are described as resembling a maze. In the third act Gonzalo, wearying of the quest for Ferdinand which has taken them across the island, begs for a respite: "Here's a maze trod indeed," he laments, "Through forthrights and meanders" (3.3.2–3). Later Alonso, speaking not of physical but of mental peregrinations, remarks on seeing the ship and its crew restored,

> This is as strange a maze as e'er men trod,
> And there is in this business more than nature
> Was ever conduct of.
>
> (5.1.242–44)

The use of the word "maze" here is particularly striking, because it is a word which otherwise appears only three times in all of Shakespeare, once each in two early plays, and once in an early poem (*The Taming of the Shrew* 1.2.55; *A Midsummer Night's Dream* 2.1.99; *The Rape of Lucrece*, 1151). Furthermore, the etymologically related word "amazement" appears an additional three times, in positions which frame the action of the drama. Thus in 1.1 Prospero seeks to assure Miranda that all is well, so that she need feel "no more amazement," while Ariel "flamed amazement" in the ship's riggings so that "Not a soul / But felt a fever of the mad." At the close of the play, in the final scene, Gonzalo exclaims wonderingly that "all torment, trouble, wonder, and amazement / Inhabits here" (5.1.104–5). In short, the characters of the play are caught in a maze which is coterminous with the play, and which is physically represented by Prospero's island, with its astonishing weather, unexpected geography, and perplexing inhabitants. Like Caliban's rock, the island confines and restrains the Neapolitan visitors, "a-mazing" them, and in the process reminding them of man's propensities for violence and sin. Even Prospero, whose "monstrosity" ironically consists in his pretension to godhead (so that the linear axis in his case becomes a circle), is confined there; as we have seen, the epilogue,

in which he asks the audience to "release me," and "set me free," lest "I
. . . be here confined by you," is only made possible by his acknowledgment
of the dangers inherent in "this rough magic," and his voluntary abdication
of power.

Although the labyrinth contains and restrains evil, it is at the same
time a work of art, whose passages, like the steps of a dance—as Jonson
observed—must be learned. And there is yet another version of the labyrinth
present in *The Tempest* which emphasizes these qualities—a visual labyrinth,
a maze presented as a maze in such a way as to form an encapsulated icon
of the entire play. It is of course the game of chess, played by Ferdinand
and Miranda, and "discovered" to the onstage and offstage audiences by
Prospero.

The selection of chess, rather than, for example, a card game or a game
of lawn bowls, is not, I think, accidental. The chessboard is a model of the
political world, in which a king, a queen, and their bishops, knights, and
pawns, are maneuvered according to different rules of movement, with the
object of capturing and checkmating the opposing king. This is very like
what has occurred in the world of Milan, where one Duke has been forcibly
replaced by another—and it is almost what has happened, twice, on the
island itself. The chess game is thus another mode of education for Ferdinand
and Miranda, who are preparing to return to the world of ongoing social
action as King and Queen of Naples.

On the other hand, chess is a game—and a game with elaborate rules.
In this sense it is an artifact analogous not only to the maze, which in
England is traditionally the site of a variety of lawn games, but also to the
play itself; whether the rules are set by Shakespeare or by Prospero, each
piece moves a different way toward a desired and predetermined end. In
the play, as on the board, many characters are checked, or brought to a
standstill. Ferdinand is spellbound and immobilized; the king and his fol-
lowers are "confined together" in the lione-grove by Ariel, where "they
cannot budge till [Prospero's] release" (5.1.7–11). Often indirection brings
about desired movements, and the compact model of the chessboard serves
as a microcosm within the microcosm, picturing the dominion of king and
queen and the interplay of black and white squares: good and evil, black
magic and white, the hegemony of Sycorax and that of Prospero. As Ferdinand and Miranda master the game of chess, they retrace their steps
through the play, noting its inherent dangers, and displaying the knowledge
which will protect them from the fate of either an Icarus or a Minotaur.
For the essence of the contest is the acknowledgement that there are both
kinds of squares, black and white, and that opposition and emulation are
part of the rules of the game.

In our schematization, we have thus far neglected the crucial enclosing labyrinth which is the play itself, and the natural questers who are the audience. We, like Gonzalo and other naifs, are struck with "amazement" as the drama unfolds, showing us the shipwreck, the nuptial pageant, and the spectacle of the "three men of sin." From first to last, the audience is an intrinsic part of the action. Significantly, however, we are not cast as gods, nor as monsters—nor are we even artists, Daedaluses or Prosperos, who make things happen. All of these attitudes are fully circumscribed by the play, and each is endowed with its full complement of hazards. The audience, however, is invited to play a different role, and a role entirely consonant with the spirit of the play. For we are not gods but heroes, men and women pressed to the utmost of our human capabilities—we are Theseuses finding our way with caution and exhilaration through the corridors of an art which is at once definable as craft and being. But if we are Theseuses, Shakespeare is our Ariadne, and the thread by which he guides us out of the maze is the very matrix of thematic patterns we have already noted. For us, as for Ferdinand, it is crucial that we should perceive man's plenitude and his boundaries; for us, as for Miranda, it is essential that we should choose between the two suitors, a monster and a seeming god, and accept the man who is always somewhere between them. *The Tempest* is many things—but not least among those things, it is Shakespeare's extraordinary version of the Daedalus myth.

At the last, the play offers its audience a choice between one kind of wonder and another—between "Miranda," the "wondered at," and Caliban, the "monster," the divine portent or warning. With characteristic humanity, the Renaissance *via media*, Shakespeare demonstrates to us the poles of god and beast, and permits us to choose. Over one hundred years earlier, Pico della Mirandola spoke confidently about the nature of such a choice: "We have made thee," he has his God tell Adam, "neither of heaven nor of earth, neither mortal nor immortal, so that with freedom of choice and with honor, as though the maker and molder of thyself in whatever shape thou shalt prefer. Thou shalt have the power to degenerate into the lower forms of life, which are brutish. Thou shalt have the power, out of thy soul's judgment, to be reborn into higher forms, which are divine." Pico's world was more optimistic than Shakespeare's, though it shared the same parameters. For *The Tempest* affirms the necessity of a choice, not of bestiality or godhead, but of something, everything, in between—a choice, as Wallace Stevens wrote, "not between, but of."

Learning to Curse: Linguistic Colonialism in *The Tempest*

Stephen J. Greenblatt

In *The Tempest* the startling encounter between a lettered and an unlettered culture is heightened, almost parodied, in the relationship between a European whose entire source of power is his library and a savage who had no speech at all before the European's arrival. "Remember / First to possess his books," Caliban warns the lower-class and presumably illiterate Stephano and Trinculo,

> for without them
> He's but a sot, as I am, nor hath not
> One spirit to command: they all do hate him
> As rootedly as I. Burn but his books.

This idea may well have had some historical analogue in the early years of conquest. In his *Thresor de l'histoire des langves de cest univers* (1607), Claude Duret reports that the Indians, fearing that their secrets would be recorded and revealed, would not approach certain trees whose leaves the Spanish used for paper, and Father Chaumonot writes in 1640 that the Hurons "were convinced that we were sorcerers, imposters come to take possession of their country, after having made them perish by our spells which were shut up in our inkstands, in our books, etc.,—inasmuch that we dared not, without hiding ourselves, open a book or write anything."

The link between *The Tempest* and the New World has often been

From *First Images of America: The Impact of the New World on the Old,* vol. 2, edited by Fredi Chiappelli. © 1976 by the Regents of the University of California. University of California Press, 1976.

noted, most recently by Terence Hawkes who suggests, in his book *Shake-speare's Talking Animals,* that in creating Prospero, the playwright's imagination was fired by the resemblance he perceived between himself and a colonist. "A colonist," write Hawkes,

> acts essentially as a dramatist. He imposes the "shape" of his own culture, *embodied in his speech,* on the new world, and makes that world recognizable, habitable, "natural," able to speak his language.

Conversely,

> the dramatist is metaphorically a colonist. His art penetrates new areas of experience, his language expands the boundaries of our culture, and makes the new territory over in its own image. His "raids on the inarticulate" open up new worlds for the imagination.

To read such glowing tribute, one would never know that there had been a single doubt whispered in the twentieth century about the virtues of European colonialism. More important, one would never know that Prospero and the other Europeans leave the island at the end of the play. If *The Tempest* is holding up a mirror to colonialism, Shakespeare is far more ambivalent than Terence Hawkes about the reflected image.

Caliban enters in act 1, cursing Prospero and protesting bitterly: "This island's mine, by Sycorax my mother, / Which thou tak'st from me" (1. 2.333–34). When he first arrived, Prospero made much of Caliban, and Caliban, in turn, showed Prospero "all the qualities o'th'isle." But now, Caliban complains, "I am all the subjects that you have, / Which first was mine own King." Prospero replies angrily that he had treated Caliban "with human care" until he tried to rape Miranda, a charge Caliban does not deny. At this point, Miranda herself chimes in, with a speech Dryden and others have found disturbingly indelicate:

> Abhorred slave,
> Which any print of goodness wilt not take,
> Being capable of all ill! I pitied thee,
> Took pains to make thee speak, taught thee each hour
> One thing or other: when thou didst not, savage,
> Know thine own meaning, but wouldst gabble like
> A thing most brutish, I endow'd thy purposes
> With words that made them known. But thy vile race,

Though thou didst learn, had that in't which good natures
Could not abide to be with; therefore wast thou
Deservedly confin'd into this rock,
Who hadst deserv'd more than a prison.

To this, Caliban replies:

You taught me language; and my profit on't
Is, I know how to curse. The red plague rid you
For learning me your language!

(1.2.353–67)

Caliban's retort might be taken as self-indictment: even with the gift of language, his nature is so debased that he can only learn to curse. But the lines refuse to mean this; what we experience instead is a sense of their devastating justness. Ugly, rude, savage, Caliban nevertheless achieves for an instant an absolute, if intolerably bitter, moral victory. There is no reply; only Prospero's command: "Hag-seed, hence! / Fetch us in fuel," coupled with an ugly threat:

If thou neglect'st, or dost unwillingly
What I command, I'll rack thee with old cramps,
Fill all thy bones with aches, make thee roar,
That beasts shall tremble at thy din.

(1.2.370–73)

What makes this exchange so powerful, I think, is that Caliban is anything but a Noble Savage. Shakespeare does not shrink from the darkest European fantasies about the Wild Man; indeed he exaggerates them: Caliban is deformed, lecherous, evil-smelling, idle, treacherous, naive, drunken, rebellious, violent, and devil-worshipping. According to Prospero, he is not even human: a "born devil," "got by the devil himself / Upon thy wicked dam" (1.2.321–22). *The Tempest* utterly rejects the uniformitarian view of the human race, the view that would later triumph in the Enlightenment and prevail in the West to this day. All men, the play seems to suggest, are *not* alike; strip away the adornments of culture and you will *not* reach a single human essence. If anything, *The Tempest* seems closer in spirit to the attitude of the present-day inhabitants of Java who, according to Clifford Geertz, quite flatly say, "To be human is to be Javanese" (*The Interpretation of Cultures*).

And yet out of the midst of this attitude Caliban wins a momentary victory that is, quite simply, an assertion of inconsolable human pain and bitterness. And out of the midst of this attitude Prospero comes, at the end of the play, to say of Caliban, "this thing of darkness I / Acknowledge mine" (5.1.275–76). Like Caliban's earlier reply, Prospero's words are ambiguous; they might be taken as a bare statement that the strange "demi-devil" is one of Prospero's party as opposed to Alonso's, or even that Caliban is Prospero's slave. But again the lines refuse to mean this: they acknowledge a deep, if entirely unsentimental, bond. By no means is Caliban accepted into the family of man; rather, he is claimed as Philoctetes might claim his own festering wound. Perhaps, too, the word "acknowledge" implies some moral responsibility, as when the Lord, in the King James translation of Jeremiah, exhorts men to "acknowledge thine iniquity, that thou hast transgressed against the Lord thy God" (3:13). Certainly the Caliban of act 5 is in a very real sense Prospero's creature, and the bitter justness of his retort early in the play still casts a shadow at its close. With Prospero restored to his dukedom, the match of Ferdinand and Miranda blessed, Ariel freed to the elements, and even the wind and tides of the return voyage settled, Shakespeare leaves Caliban's fate naggingly unclear. Prospero has acknowledged a bond; that is all.

The Tempest as Supplement

Julian Patrick

The conspicuous dominance of middle states in narrative and dramatic romance (always after the before and usually before the after) tends to suppress what in other genres we recognize as the specific nature of beginnings and the finality of endings. Beginnings in romance are often resumptions, and endings are sometimes ironic or abrupt when they are not endless. Thus the true centre of romance cannot be in plot or character, as it must be in tragedy and realistic fiction, where the moment of the beginning is greatly emphasized, but rather in the retrospective and prospective movement of implication in the action. In romance, past and future are continually being woven together in the present space of narrative, or of dramatic re-presentation. In the *Odyssey,* for instance, the island of Scheria, land of the Phaiakians, is middled, as it were, by its complicated set of dual relations: between past and future, between the gods on serene Olympus and the suffering of shipwrecked Odysseus, between Poseidon's ship of stone and the craftsmanship of stone and the craftsmanship of Athene. Scheria is also the place where Odysseus tells the story of his wanderings and where (through the meeting with Nausicaa, the repudiation of the haughty Phaiakian prince, and the show of strength with the massive discus) he prepares for the return to Penelope, his battle with the suitors, and the test of strength with the great bow. If we allow Calypso's isle to stand for all the islands that precede it in the chronology of the story (the island near

From *Centre and Labyrinth: Essays in Honour of Northrop Frye,* edited by Eleanor Cook, Chaviva Hosek, Jay Macpherson, Patricia Parker, and Julian Patrick. © 1983 by the University of Toronto Press.

the Cyclopo's home, the island of Aeolus, Circe's island, the island of Thrinacia, etc.), then the *Odyssey* is a romance of islands, the middle space of wandering, being succeeded by the middle space of tale-telling, which gives way to the middle space of return. The ending is itself a middle, for Tiresias's prophecy to Odysseus of another journey inland to a place where the sea is unknown carries the imagination forward and beyond the abrupt ending that Athena's recalling of Odysseus to the seat of justice and political responsibility gives to the story.

Because the middle states of romances are both unstable and actively generative, works like the *Odyssey* and *The Tempest* have naturally attracted to themselves two different but related kinds of elaboration. As is well known, the reception of the *Odyssey* in classical times took the form either of relentless allegorizing of its many suggestive episodes, or of the continuation of its action by later romancers—as if the plot must mean more than it says, or, in order to mean at all, it must be made to say more. It is interesting that the same two procedures also characterize the reception of *The Tempest*: a brief examination of their characteristic strategies will help to define the subtle and complex relation between forms of supplementary elaboration and the structure of *The Tempest*.

We can see what this structure is, and why it needs supplementary elaboration, at the moment when the structure begins to come apart in Prospero's conspicuous feeling of release, at the beginning of the fifth act, from the demands of dramatic production:

> Now does my project gather to a head
> My charms crack not; my spirits obey; and Time
> Goes upright with his carriage.
>
> (5.1.1–3)

Like the theatre-audience at the end of the play, Time can now begin to stand up straight because he has very little left to carry (to do). Unlike *The Winter's Tale,* which brought Time on stage to explain what the dramatic action has to leave out, *The Tempest* thinks of Time as supporting the entire action. And, of course, it does, in the literal sense that the theatre-audience has been in the theatre for the length of time that the court party has been on the island. But the personification also implies, less literally, that what time has supported has been a metaphor *for* time, that time in the play is to be understood *as* the various actions that the characters have undergone. Thus, it is at this moment, in the several meetings of the court party with Miranda and Ferdinand and with Caliban and his friends, that the various "times" of the many subplot actions become the one, continuous and human time of Prospero's re-formed society. The final recognition, or meeting, takes place between Prospero and the theatre-audience, when Prospero implies that, in order to be released from his dramatic role, he needs the audience to understand the action he had built up for them. As Prospero has forgiven the court party, as Ferdinand and his father have mutually exchanged forgiveness, as Caliban has sought the same quality, so the audience, once they understand what they have seen (for the other acts of forgiveness were based on understanding, that is, on recognition) will also forgive, as Prospero has done, by responding. Understanding and mutual acknowledgment, then, gradually supplement and substitute for the bleaker knowledge of human nature embodied in Ariel's speech to the "three men of sin" and in Prospero's disgusted repudiation of Caliban after the masque of Ceres. It is for this reason—to allow the time of human understanding to supplement the objectified and articulated structure of time that the audience has just witnessed in the main action of the play—that the shape of the fifth act is dominated by its incomplete, fragile, and perilous mergings and its delicate suspensions. The action cannot close definitively because its real closure lies in the imaginative capacity and commitment of the theatre-audience.

Yet it is very easy to imagine an audience who would lack such an understanding. For it, the action of *The Tempest* would close perilously only to open again as the romance imagination continued to wonder about the journey home to Milan and to the problems awaiting Prospero in his human, all-too-human, form. Thus, for F. G. Waldron in *The Virgin Queen . . . a Sequel to Shakespeare's "Tempest"* (1797), Shakespeare's ending is clearly a mistake. On the voyage home, the spirit of Sycorax, inflamed by love for her darling Caliban, rises again and is only prevented from destroying Prospero's homecoming by the sudden arrival, in the very nick of time, of Ariel, who is carrying Prospero's once drowned book and his now carefully mended staff. The lessons Prospero learns this second time are those he should have learned the first: leave the bad characters behind on the island and keep your supernatural guns beside you.

Prospero's staff is also important to another form in which *The Tempest* begins to be rewritten by nineteenth-century men of letters. This is the interpretation of *The Tempest* as an autobiographical allegory, as an announcement to London theatre-goers that its author is abandoning the stage and returning to Stratford whence he came some twenty-four years before: "Here Shakespeare himself is Prospero, or rather the superior genius who commands both Prospero and Ariel. But the time was approaching when the potent sorcerer was to break his staff, and to bury it fathoms in the ocean. . . . That staff has never been, and never will be, recovered (1838)."

The implied contrast between the romancers and the allegorists is very interesting. Waldron's romantic impulse to rewrite the plot by continuing it past its point of closure is connected to a desire to free the action from the pressure of its informing ideas, recognition of which alone can make the ending satisfactory. The allegorists, in contrast, by fixing the significance of the action through its supposed autobiographical reference, ignore the play's constantly changing focus and turn its plot into pure repetition. Yet the play is as insistently allegorizable as its action is romantic. In what follows, the various manifest patterns of its structure, especially those which connect the dramatization of time with the play's many audiences, will be used to clarify the relation of the action of *The Tempest* to its systematic play of ideas.

I

Shakespeare begins both the narrated story of *The Tempest* and the dramatic action with an image of time. Antonio has usurped his brother Prospero's throne because he thought Prospero incapable of "temporal royalties" (1.2.110); and, in the opening shipwreck of the dramatic action, the terrible tempest is connected with the recovery of, among other things, temporal power, *tempestas* meaning both time and storm in Latin. Usurpation and its consequences—the division of spiritual from temporal royalties—and the awareness of time itself are closely connected in Shakespeare's earlier dramatic practice. In many of his usurpation or substitution plays, time itself arises as a concept reflecting an interruption to the normal order of things. It is as if time would not exist were the rhythm of ordinary measurement not altered. The periodic and ceaseless rhythms of alternating phenomena, the sun setting and rising, the lunar cycle, the change of the seasons, the round of the year, and especially the systolic and diastolic motion of the heart felt in the pulse and the intake and expulsion of air in breathing, all these phenomena "measure" time in its ordinary and "timeless" appearances. Once these rhythms are interrupted, as in the eclipse of the sun-king by the storms of usurpation in *Richard II*, or, more subtly, by what Miranda calls the "beating in [her] mind" of the pulse, which we associate with an extreme emotional identification, then the observer can become aware of time itself, as an idea that somehow reflects the interruption. In many of Shakespeare's substitution plays, usurpation and time are also connected with self-consciousness and theatrical representation. Thus, when Prospero's brother Antonio is described as a trusted substitute or supplement for Prospero (1.2.103), when this metaphor is added to one drawn from music ("having both the key / Of officer and office, set all hearts i'th'state / To what tune pleased his ear, that now he was / The ivy which had hid my princely trunk" [1.2.83–86]) and when, finally, Antonio's usurpation is described in a metaphor drawn from acting ("Hence his ambition growing— / . . . / To have no screen between this part he played / And him he played it for" [1.2.105–8]), it is clear that the play's concern with usurpation, time, representation, and self-consciousness links it with earlier plays and leads us to expect that Prospero's action will take a dramatic shape, by appealing to the imagination through the forms of time itself.

What the forms of time precisely are might seem hopelessly abstract or vague were it not for the almost unfathomable suggestiveness of *The Tempest* with regard to time. That *The Tempest*'s action is largely about time is suggested by the usually disregarded importance to the narrative frame of Claribel, the daughter of Alonzo, King of Naples. Antonio's power in Milan has been secured by taking momentary advantage of Prospero's secret studies. Milan is now a vassal state of Naples and must take its political direction, not from Prospero's knowledge of the liberal arts, but by following the purposeless lead of Alonzo. That Alonzo's leadership is without direction, even defeatist, is demonstrated by the fact that there is no good reason for the court party to be on the high seas at the moment the play opens. They are returning from the wedding of Alonzo's daughter, Claribel, to the king of Tunis; but this is a marriage no one has wanted, least of all Claribel, who has protested it bitterly. The marriage means that Claribel is as good as dead, being outside time as it is normally measured, and with the supposed death of Ferdinand in the shipwreck, the disinheriting of Naples appears to be complete: "Claribel," says Antonio when he tempts Sebastian to help with the murder of Alonzo,

> is Queen of Tunis; she that dwells
> Ten leagues beyond man's life; she that from Naples
> Can have no note, unless the sun were post—
> The Man i'th'Moon's too slow—till new born chins
> Be rough and razorable; she that from whom
> We all were sea-swallow'd, though some cast again
> (And by that destiny) to perform an act
> Whereof what's past is prologue, what to come
> In yours and my discharge.
>
> (2.1.246–54)

This deeply ironic description connects the machiavel-actor's dependency on momentary opportunities—the temporal illusion that now is the right moment, that the door is opening—with a consequent imprisonment within

fate or destiny itself. The passage makes us see the connection between
political power *in* time, mere "temporal royalties," and the ideal possibilities
of time, which it will be the task of Prospero's art to represent. When
Gonzalo discovers that Ferdinand and Miranda are betrothed to be married,
he expresses for the audience our sense that the action, in joining Ferdinand
to Miranda, has reconnected temporal royalties with the larger royalties of
art and thus has made sense, finally, of Claribel's marriage: "In one voyage
/ Did Claribel her husband find at Tunis, / And Ferdinand, her brother,
found a wife / Where he himself was lost; Prospero, his dukedom / In a
poor isle; and all of us, ourselves, / When no man was his own"
(5.1.208–13).

   This "bountifull" conjunction of fortunes on the island suggests why
the play's third scene, in which the court party talks desultorily about their
luck in escaping from the shipwreck, takes the shape it does. The scene
expounds symbolically the attitudes of mind that have underlain past events
and, in this sense, it parallels Prospero's exposition of his own past to
Miranda in the scene before. In precisely opposed attitudes to political time,
Gonzalo dreams of establishing on the island a government "t'excell the
Golden Age" while Antonio dreams of assassination. The attempt to escape
from time in a fantasy of perfection is as useless as Antonio's ignoring of
all but the most brutal of time's uses is self-regarding. The scene as a whole,
with its desultory meandering dialogue, its mention of Widow Dido
and Aeneas and Tunis and Carthage, is meant to be understood by us as a
kind of temporizing, or playing for time, and to suggest that court life,
without Prospero's knowledge of the liberal arts, could be only fantasy or
plotting.

   The opposite of this temporizing is Prospero's concentrated and at
times agonized attention on every aspect of the island-stage, from getting
the timing right for Ferdinand and Miranda's first meeting, to the slow-
time of Alonzo's search for Ferdinand through the labyrinth of loss and
guilt. Prospero's control over the rising action of the play can be understood
as a combination of three analogies of ordinary temporal experience: events
that follow one another in time, or succession; events that occur at the same
time, or simultaneity; and events that recur, or permanence. Succession is
conveyed by the fact that each of the three dramatic subplots has its own
sequence of events, each with its own temporal pace—very slow, for the
court party; neither slow nor fast, for the comic subplot of Caliban (for
whom the illusion is created that he is proceeding at his own sweet pace);
and faster than the blink of an eye for the lovers. Each sequence leads to a
climactic vision and each of these visions disappears, to be replaced by a

form of punishment, or, in the case of the lovers, by Prospero's "revels" speech, which hastens to explain what could be regarded as a punishment, the loss of paradise.

If the experience of time as succession appears to divide the three groups from one another in the mind of the audience, the experience of time as simultaneity brings each group into significant association with the others. For the court party, Ferdinand is a lost heir, forever sunk beneath the seas. For Miranda, by contrast, he has been born from the seas and has found in Prospero a second father. Alonzo seeks Ferdinand in the muddy depths of the ocean; Ferdinand seeks to remain in paradise forever. Antonio's "strong imagination" sees a crown dropping upon Sebastian's head, while Caliban tries to make Stephano king of the island. The final crown, as Gonzalo notes, belongs to the young lovers:

> Look down, you gods,
> And on this couple drop a blessed crown!
> For it is you that have chalk'd forth the way
> Which brought us hither.
>
> (5.2.201–4)

These overlapping simultaneities reach their climax in the recognition scene, when the experience of the whole cast is defined in terms of degrees of conscious awareness, extending from the ship's crew, who have slept through the action, to Antonio and Sebastian, whose constant wakefulness is an index both of their scheming and of their blindness to imaginative experience. In between are the great dreamers of the action, Caliban, Gonzalo, the young lovers, and Prospero himself, whose own vision of paradise makes him forget the persistence of Caliban's foolish plot. Perhaps the most telling of simultaneities concerns the concept of plot. The plotting of Antonio, like that of Caliban, is defeated, but so is the "plot" (4.1.88) of Venus and Cupid against the chastity of the young lovers. In its place we find the "grass-plot," the "very place" to which Ceres is invited "to come and sport" (4.1.73–74). Here the original meaning of "plot" as a piece of land replaces its derived meaning, as a scheming in time, as a vision of paradise replaces an action in time, as a masque momentarily is substituted for a dramatic plot.

The experience of time as permanence is expressed in the masque of Ceres with its symbolic presentation of the *ver perpetuum* as a promise of fertility. The permanence of certain aspects of experience, in this case of earliest memories, is also suggested in the masque by a beautifully inobvious repetition. To her father's great surprise, Miranda is able to remember the four or five gentlewomen who tended her before in Milan (1.2.44–47); this shadowy memory is given a permanent form in art by the goddesses Iris, Ceres, and Juno, who attend Miranda's betrothal.

II

To describe Prospero's art by means of these three analogies of time is to give some idea of how the complex temporal organization of the play is made to substitute for a more straightforward kind of dramatic action, but it cannot suggest the representational power of the three subplots— how they are related to conceptions of human time—nor how we are to understand Prospero's acute sense of crisis, his "zenith" which "depend[s] upon / A most auspicious star, whose influence / If now I court not, but omit, my fortunes / Will ever after droop" (1.2.181–84). It has been noticed that the word "now" is used more often in *The Tempest* than in any other play of Shakespeare. It is also significant that the longest stretch of dialogue in which the word is not used comes in the middle of the scene of temporizing action in which Gonzalo dreams and Antonio begins the temptation of Sebastian. For Caliban, who, by contrast, shares Prospero's sense of crisis, the time for Prospero's murder is "now," because at this time, mid-afternoon, it is Prospero's custom to sleep. One way to kill Prospero, Caliban suggest, is to drive a nail through his head as he sleeps. He must have in mind the temple of the skull, the place where the skull is weakest and where the pulse, the chronometer of the body, can be seen most easily.

We associate, however, the use of the word "now," together with the sense of crisis, of being burdened by time, with Prospero. It is this sense of time as crisis-time through which Prospero is most clearly related to Ariel and most clearly distinguished from him. Ariel's joy as Prospero's helper is to enact in spectacular dramatic form the thoughts of his master. Thus, we can understand Ariel as the spirit of instantaneous imaginative embodiment, as quick as thought itself, the spirit that, in the famous terms of Theseus's speech in *A Midsummer Night's Dream,* makes "apprehension" into "comprehension" because "such tricks hath strong imagination / That, if it would apprehend some joy / It comprehends some bringer of that joy" (5.1.18–20). Joy and freedom, those large apprehendable abstracts, are brought into the range of human comprehension and made temporal by words, the means by which air is given human, communicable shape. This is why Prospero, when he promises Ariel his freedom, says "Thou shalt be as free as mountain winds: but then exactly do / All points of my command" and why Ariel replies, "to the syllable" (1.2.501–3). Northrop Frye remarks that although there are cyclical symbols deriving from the seasons, the round of the day, the evaporation and condensation of water, and the movement of the stars, "there is no cycle of air: the wind bloweth where it listeth and images dealing with the movement of 'spirit' are likely to be associated with the theme of unpredictability or sudden crisis." Surely, then, Ariel is that winged spirit of creation that comes in response to a moment of crisis or imagined failure, but because the spirit he represents is not cyclical, it is not really human either and is capable at any moment, and especially when the crisis has passed, of disappearing "into air, into thin air" (4.1.150).

In a play so obsessed with the structures and phenomena of time, it is not surprising that Ariel's dispersal of the various groups from the ship "in troops . . . about the isle" (1.2.220) should be precisely related to distinct aspects of time, that we should see in the very fact of the three subplots a division of human time itself into its constituent aspects, the past, present, and future. The action of the court party on the island reflects a progressive realization that their life especially is founded upon repetition. Thus, when Alonzo's labyrinthine search for his lost son Ferdinand is finally concluded by Prospero's description of him as a man of sin, Alonzo's response to this new knowledge suggests that Ferdinand has always been lost because born to such a father and that his drowning is for Alonzo a culmination:

> O, it is monstrous, monstrous!
> Methought the billows spoke, and told me of it;
> The winds did sing it to me, and the thunder,
> That deep and dreadful organ-pipe, pronounc'd
> The name of Prosper; it did bass my trespass.
> Therefore my son i' th' ooze is bedded; and
> I'll seek him deeper than e'er plummet sounded,
> And with him there lie mudded.
>
> (3.3.95–102)

The sounds of this remarkable passage together form an iconic duplication of the way in which Alonzo's linear, but maze-like and repetitive, search for Ferdinand keeps deepening, as it continues, into an image of the significance of the search. The apparently casual alliteration in the first two lines (the first, innocent indication of repetition) becomes progressively undergirded by the clustering towards the speech's end of words with double consonants or vowels ("Bass," "trespass," "ooze," "bedded," "seek," "deeper," "plummet," "mudded"), so that the principle of alliteration itself, as mere repetition of sound in time, becomes accused by a deeper sound.

If the activities of the court party on the island represent the falling back of what is only apparently a present moment into a representation of the past, making the provision of allegorical icons, like the disappearing banquet and the representation of Ariel as a harpy, psychologically appropriate to such a state, the dramatization of Caliban, Trinculo, and Stephano follows the opposite procedure. They are made by their actions to represent a present moment that will not become future despite Caliban's persistent attempts to organize Trinculo and Stephano into an assassination plot. For this reason we do not hear anything about Stephano's and Trinculo's arrival on the island until we see Trinculo discovering Caliban in the act of hiding from him. Because Shakespeare has not prepared the audience for this sudden encounter, the action of the comic figures tends to suggest a kind of pure present whose temporal relations to past and future become, despite Caliban's efforts, virtually irrelevant. Prospero is able to divert the assassination attempt by hanging theatrical costumes on the clothesline for Stephano and Trinculo to dress up in, like adult-children unable to imagine anything more than present gratification. Hence, when Ariel comes to lead the comic characters to their punishment, he changes costume, appearing now as a piper playing on a drum and leading Stephano and Trinculo off stage as if at the head of a parade, the very index of present-centred activity.

If the first two subplots can be described, respectively, as a present that forfeits the quality of being present by repeating the past and as a present that remains present in its very obliviousness to other temporal modes, the love of Ferdinand and Miranda represents a present preserved so that it can ensure the arrival of a future. This is one of the functions of Prospero's irritable and alienating emphasis upon Miranda's virginity, as we can see by comparing once again the play's three conspiracies. The conspiracy of Antonio against Alonzo, by being prevented, is made to mirror the usurpation of Prospero twelve years before. The way Caliban's conspiracy is prevented makes it mirror his present frustration at what he thinks is Prospero's abuse. But the conspiracy, or "plot," of Venus against the young lovers fails and is replaced by a symbolic vision of married chastity and the fertility traditionally associated with it.

This suggests that the three subplots are being systematically related to one another. It is certainly clear that each is based on a different cluster of dramatic conventions—on allegorized narrative for the court party, on the *lazzi* and character conventions of the *commedia dell'arte* for the Caliban subplot, and on varieties of pastoral for the young lovers. But it is also true that the three subplots are based on distinct semiotic systems. C. S. Peirce's trichotomization of the linguistic sign into icon, index, and symbol is anticipated by the signs Shakespeare has chosen for his three subplots and perhaps explains why we feel, intuitively, that they go together so well. Iconic signs, as the word "icon" suggests, are signs which contain within themselves actualizations of the object or referent to which they refer, or, in more neutral language, that possess by similarity or analogy the properties of the thing they denote. Thus, Ariel as a harpy is an iconic sign, an allegory of, or metaphor for, greedy desires which spoil what they touch. Indexal signs are not like their objects, as in the previous case; instead, they point dynamically to their objects because they are related to them metonymically. Thus Ariel as a drummer leading what amounts to a parade can be understood as pointing to the activity that best characterizes the comic subplot. The relation between the sign and its object is unmotivated for symbolic signs; there is nothing about a symbolic sign that necessarily connects it to its object. Symbolic signs are therefore culture-specific and their meaning has to be learned. Ariel as Iris presenting the masque of Ceres for Miranda and Ferdinand refers to the rainbow that comes after waters recede; but this association has to be learned (unlike harpies, who are, simply, harpyish, and drummers, who drum). Peirce himself recognized the different temporal registers of his division: "an icon has such being as belongs to past experience. An index has the being of present experience. The being of a symbol is *esse in futuro.*"

III

The Tempest, with its haunting repetitions and its totalizing picture of human time, has the capacity to remind us of our earliest needs and desires because its subject is the losses and gains of a whole lifetime seen from the perspective of Prospero, who is portrayed as alone having the power and wisdom to re-create the image of a whole society. Two extraordinary dramatic spectacles, the beginning shipwreck and the masque of Ceres, as they dissolve in front of our eyes, dissolve also in front of their principal spectators, Miranda and Prospero. Even after Prospero's explanation of their expulsion from Milan, Miranda does not understand the reason for raising the sea-storm (it is the beginning of time for her) and asks her father to explain it "for still 'tis beating in my mind" (1.2.176). By contrast, the masque of Ceres begins to vanish when Prospero remembers that the moment of Caliban's plot has almost arrived (it is a premonition of the end of time for him). Accordingly, he consoles Ferdinand and Miranda for their loss of paradise and tries to control his own emotions: "a turn or two I'll walk, / To still my beating mind" (4.1.161–62). In turn, this important echo reminds us of the extremely close relations in this play between the spectacle produced and the audience watching.

This is emphasized by the fact that, as has often been remarked, *The Tempest* keeps to the unity of time. We learn very quickly that the duration of the imagined action on the island will be identical to the time spent by the audience in the theatre. The care and with with which this illusion is established makes us acutely conscious of the relation between the on-stage action and the theatre audience, since what is happening to the characters is, in temporal terms at least, the same as what is happening to us.

Thus, because *The Tempest* begins with a tempest, that is, with an event that actually appears to be happening right in front of us and is not mediated by a preparatory event of any kind, it is as if we were being hurried right into the centre of time itself as we see a whole society, from King to sailor, apparently being destroyed. But when Miranda and Prospero appear before us, suspending our sense of the inevitability of loss and death and replacing it with a complex action to rebuild the destroyed society according to ideal norms, the result is that the theatre audience is displaced from its privileged position as the central spectator of the action. It is not only displaced, it is made marginal by this movement from nature to art and from action to contemplation. From now on, until almost the very end of the play, what happens on stage happens to other audiences than us, as we watch others being watched.

By studying Miranda's response to the shipwreck, we can gain some understanding of the paradoxical position of the audience of *The Tempest*, linked by time to the on-stage events but displaced by the apparent motive and direction of those events:

> If by your art, my dearest father, you have
> Put the wild waters in this roar, allay them.
> The sky it seems would pour down stinking pitch,
> But that the sea, mounting to th' welkin's cheek,
> Dashes the fire out. O! I have suffered
> With those that I saw suffer. A brave vessel
> (Who had, no doubt, some noble creature in her)
> Dash'd all to pieces! O, the cry did knock
> Against my very heart. Poor souls, they perish'd.
> Had I been any God of power, I would
> Have sunk the sea within the earth or ere
> It should the good ship so have swallow'd, and
> The fraughting souls within her.
>
> (1.2.1–13)

What is striking about this speech is the division between father and daughter that threatens to open in Miranda's protest at the loss of the "fraughting souls" and which is implied by her indirect identification of her father as a god of power who could have prevented the storm had he wished. To sink the sea within the earth, as Miranda suggests, is the opposite of what Antonio and Sebastian satirically suggest that Gonzalo would do with the island on which they have found themselves:

> ANTONIO: What impossible matter will he make easy next?
> SEBASTIAN: I think he will carry this island home in his pocket,
>   and give it his son for an apple.
> ANTONIO: And sowing the kernels of it in the sea, bring forth
>   more islands.

> (2.1.89–94)

To fertilize the sea with islands is to expand the earth within the sea, to plant the sea and make it grow. Hence, both Miranda's response to the shipwreck and the implied response of Gonzalo to the island deny one-half of the sea's essential nature, its separating and dividing force that causes loss and death. And each leads in the direction suggested by the whole structure of the play, towards the experience of the unexpected supplement to time that lies buried in the very nature of imaginative response. Miranda's response to the shipwreck is genuinely supplementary in the sense that her speech implicitly expresses a knowledge of something that we, the theatre audience, do not yet know. For the noble souls are not dead and Miranda's surmise of herself as a god of power is the imaginative form which that intuitive knowledge takes. There is, then, a sense in which Miranda's response precedes the shipwreck, and is a version of the cry and smile that preserved her father when they were expelled onto the sea twelve years before. The supplementary quality of Miranda's response is confirmed by the miraculous retention in her memory of the image of "four or five women who once tended her" (1.2.46–47). Her memory forges the first link with the past experience in Milan and is thus the first sign that there are indeed islands to be sown in the sea of time.

Prospero, of course, is not a god of power, as his troubled exposition of his past, his anger at Caliban's conspiracy, and his "human" forgiveness of his enemies make very clear; only his "art," the art of constructing an image of time, makes him appear as one for most of the action. He is not a god of power because the action of *The Tempest* is not exclusively the re-creation of human society according to ideal models; it is also for Prospero his own reentry into the stream of human experience. This becomes clear at the end of the masque of Ceres, when Prospero forgets the approach of

Caliban's conspiracy because he is so involved in the spectacle he is producing for Ferdinand and Miranda. Caliban moves him to anger, not because the conspiracy poses any threat to Prospero—it is easily dealt with—
but mainly because the movement from absorption in the spectacle of
immortality, of a year without death, to confrontation with the stupid and
vicious present, for which he is partly responsible, causes him to be reminded of time and therefore of his own mortality, a reminder perhaps
always implicit in the movement of the emotions from any forgetting to
any remembering.

If Prospero is not a god of power and must continually be reminded
of his human failures, time is not immortal either and the ideal vision of
the masque of Ceres, though not questioned as art, is questioned in its
relevance to what we have been calling the "whole of life." The "revels"
speech consoles the lovers for the loss of their vision of perfection, but the
form the consolation takes is to predict the final disappearance of time for
the observer. Thus the question is raised, what is left over from the vision,
what could supplement the loss of such a perfect fusion of art and nature
as the masque of Ceres has presented? A partial answer comes from watching
how Shakespeare manages the gradual and beautiful disengagement from
the dream world on the island. Whether we think of this disengagement
as the image of the illusory spirits disappearing, or as Prospero's renunciation of rough magic, or as his goodbye to Ariel, or as his successive ac-
knowledgments of Antonio, Sebastian, and Caliban, and finally the theatre
audience itself, what is clear is that, in all these successive relinquishings,
the dream world of the spirits is replaced within the frame of art by what
had appeared before to be marginal and supplementary, that is, to have
been merely an audience. That the audience gradually comes to fill up the
frame of art as its perfect illusions disappear is made clearest by Prospero's
last vanity, the display of Ferdinand and Miranda playing chess. It is significant that his "high miracle," as Sebastian calls it, has been managed
without the aid or Ariel and that Ferdinand and Miranda had been the
audience for the recent masque of Ceres. Since the lovers are "real" characters and not spirits, their appearance within the frame of art suggests both
the dependence of dramatic art (as opposed to the art of the court masque)
on images of the actual, and the reciprocal reliance on the forms of ideal
art, if it is to be recognized, of the good in human nature.

So also with Caliban. From the perspective of Prospero's knowledge
of his actions, Caliban is a born devil on whose nature nurture, or the
merely supplementary, can never stick. But now at the close even Prospero
must acknowledge what the audience has felt right along, that Caliban's

status as a minor revolutionary and would-be rapist does not represent his true value. His desire, now, to "be wise hereafter, / And seek for grace" (5.1.296–97) means that nurture has not been superfluous, or merely supplementary, but, by filling in an absence, has become necessary. Thus, beginning with the masque of Ceres, the audience in the theatre begins to sense that all the great correlative oppositions of the play, art and life, illusion and reality, contemplation and action, knowing and acknowledgment, draw strength from one another as interdependent concepts.

This, at least, is one of the implications of the original form Shakespeare gives to *The Tempest*'s epilogue. Most dramatic epilogues, including all those in other plays of Shakespeare, form a kind of second, or supplementary, ending, in which the actor who has played one of the leading roles (Puck in *A Midsummer Night's Dream*, Rosalind in *As You Like It*, to name only the two most famous instances) steps out of character and approaches the audience as an actor (often referring to himself and the rest of the cast as actors, as Puck does). In this convention, the epilogue is a mere supplement to the main fiction, an addition or part conventionally tacked on after the action has been completed. Prospero, however, does not approach the audience as an actor but as Prospero without his magical powers; and he does not appeal wittily to the audience for their applause but seriously to the conscience and understanding of each person:

> Gentle breath of yours my sails
> Must fill, or else my project fails,
> Which was to please. Now I want
> Spirits to enforce, art to enchant,
> And my ending is despair,
> Unless I be reliev'd by prayer,
> Which pierces so, that it assaults
> Mercy itself, and frees all faults.
> As you from crimes would pardon'd be,
> Let your indulgence set me free.
> (Epilogue, ll. 11–20)

Now it is true that this epilogue follows convention in the sense that it makes an appeal to the audience to recognize that it has been well entertained by the skill of the actors. The "breath" to which Prospero refers is the comment of the audience after the performance is over, and the "prayer" the words of the epilogue. The break with convention comes within the convention itself in the seriousness of its appeal and the literalness with which it insists that only the audience's commitment to the meaning of what they have experienced will get the ship back to Naples and save Prospero from despair. Thus the epilogue is not a mere supplement to the play but its necessary conclusion, and because the epilogue has included the audience within the main action of the play, as its completion, the audience is suddenly revealed to be, not the marginal and displaced onlooker of the play, but its implied subject, its judge, and, in a way, its creator. Like death, this implied summons to the meaning of time comes from without (ends are always external to what they end); but again, like death (like the shipwreck), it has been there all along.

The Shakespearean "Metastance"

James P. Driscoll

We begin to live, Yeats observed, when we have conceived of life as a tragedy. Shakespeare's romances, expecially *The Tempest,* dramatize the truth of Yeats's dictum. To have conceived of life as a tragedy is to have gained the awareness that characterizes Lear's final Promethean stance. Lear embodies the darker side of the Promethean archetype—possession of the spirit by suffering and defiance. Prospero, who manifests its complementary brighter side—foresight, wisdom, and ability to utilize intelligence to tame nature—transcends this archetype to attain wholeness. In *The Tempest,* as in *King Lear,* destiny proves finally mysterious, providence remains a pious or naive hope, and it is up to man to better his society and life. Yet Prospero, unlike Lear, survives and accepts the tragic dimension of the human condition to achieve a higher attitude or a metastance toward Lear's tragic Promethean stance. In Prospero's metastance striving for power, secure identity, and certain belief is transcended through a choice by the whole self to live with faith in a world it knows man can never fully control or predict.

King Lear and *The Tempest* display important similarities. Betrayal and preparation for death constitute central themes in both plays; evil is radical and incorrigible in each; and each focuses on the nature of ideal identity. Moreover, Shakespeare's last romance is in many respects a direct reversal of his greatest tragedy. While Lear vainly invokes the gods to bring him justice, Prospero, through command of the spirits, secures justice for him-

From *Identity in Shakespearean Drama.* © 1983 by Associated University Presses, Inc.

self. A storm demonstrates Lear's helplessness, and a tempest dramatizes Prospero's power. Lear indirectly and unconsciously attempts to deprive his daughters of integrity and dignity. Prospero guides Miranda toward independence and frees Ariel. Cordelia's death makes it impossible for Lear to either redeem the sorrows he has felt or move beyond Promethean defiance. Miranda's life preserves Prospero from bitterness and despair, thus giving him an opportunity to attain wholeness. *King Lear* remains finally tragic because its protagonist dies possessed by his dark stance. *The Tempest* is comedic because its protagonist lives in metastance. *King Lear* posits a tragic stance toward the quest for identity and the problem of evil. *The Tempest* forms a comedic metastance to that stance.

The concept of *metastance* provides a way to explicate the peculiar mixture of skepticism and faith that marks the quintessential Shakespearean perspective. We achieve metastance when, having taken an initial stance that to our best knowledge seems valid, we stand back from our stance to gain a larger view that establishes a qualifying context. Metastance distances us from a stance without denying its range of validity. Distance allows us to maintain tolerant skepticism, which counters dogmatism, despair, and therefore hubris or ego inflation. In adopting a metastance we refuse to delimit identity through willful commitments to any stance. True metastance is characterized by skepticism and a moral or, if you will, philosophical modesty wherein we recognize the necessity of ultimately resting every stance upon a fideistic act.

Prospero's metastance to Lear's Promethean stance lies implicit in Cordelia. Prospero's transcendence of the Promethean archetype to participate in identity's highest stage makes him significantly like Cordelia. He shares her truth and inner freedom, her impatience with those who live by lies, and her willingness to accept, forgive, and act on faith. Both defy all evils that confront them, insist that others face the unpalliated truth about their real identities, yet never self-righteously assert their own goodness or implore the gods to avenge their miseries. They exhibit the harmony of truth and love and manifest the primal archetype—wholeness. As a great magician, the legendary Hermes Trismegistus's virtual incarnation, Prospero embodies two subordinate archetypes closely associated with wholeness: magician and wise old man. In accordance with the latter, he serenely prepares for the death it was Lear's tragedy to resist violently. Prospero and Cordelia are masculine and feminine, old and young, and comic and tragic embodiments of wholeness. Their ideal identity entails a metastance to both striving for identity and to the social, conscious, and real identities themselves.

Wisdom, wholeness, and metastance come to those whose recognition of radical injustice, evil, and irreparable loss enables them to conceive of life as a tragedy. Prospero's initial appreciation of life's tragic potential affords him the insight to bring events to a comic resolution. Since the early Lear, a man who believes he is everything, refuses to acknowledge the tragic dimension of the human condition, he must come to understand tragedy by living it. Those alone who have sufficient spiritual courage to eschew the egotistical fantasy of invulnerability and its corollary delusion that tragic limitations are unreal can hope to reach metastance's comedic resolution. In contrast to Christian hope, metastance offers neither the certitude that dogmatic belief entails nor the security that clearly defined identity bequeaths. Its gift is a detachment steadfast enough to permit acknowledging the possibility of unavoidable defeat and irredeemable sorrows without such acknowledgment paralyzing the will to act. Because it renders superfluous belief that the universe will prove ultimately comic, metastance allows one to live as if this were so while fully aware that it may well not be so. Hence metastance curbs man's arrogant and childish impulse to insist that the universe govern itself by human values, that the cosmos conform to a little world of cherished beliefs.

In Shakespeare characters who embrace stance unqualified by metastance and demand secure identity and certain belief display a hubris that tends to push them into moral and psychic chaos. Metastance, however, provides an Archimedean point from which a character can maintain serenity and patience when belief can no longer derive support from certain knowledge. Since Othello decidedly lacks such an Archimedean point, he cannot accommodate doubts that qualify his beliefs about his own identity and that of Desdemona. For Othello faith must be reinforced with certainties; the moment doubt undermines his rigidly held convictions, his conceptions about Desdemona's identity shatter and his identity fragments. Angelo and Isabella, with their willed purity and morality of repression, also illustrate the inflexibility common to those who lack metastance. Their need for secure identity fosters indurated personae, and their desire for certain belief nurtures a moral rigidity that inhibits and perverts love. The will to maintain an unaltering conscious identity and *persona*, as the histories and *Julius Caesar, Hamlet, Othello, Twelfth Night*, and *Measure for Measure* all show, hinders adaptation, knowledge of real identity, and progress toward wholeness. The deep self-knowledge wholeness insures forms a metastance to the stances of the social and real identity that fosters a more flexible, receptive, conscious identity.

Although the early and middle plays present many characters whose identities are founded on rigid, unqualified stances without offering characters with fully developed, compensating metastances, the metastances of Cordelia and Prospero are prefigured in Viola, Feste, Desdemona, the Duke in *Measure for Measure,* Hamlet as he achieves self-knowledge and faith, and even the mercurial early Falstaff. Metastance acquires full clarity in and after *King Lear,* where Shakespeare realizes his most profound tragic visions.

Cordelia's nothingness constitutes a metaphor for a metastance of ego-free consciousness that transcends striving for identity. Her metastance is analogous to nothingness, for she claims or asserts nothing save truth to self. Metastance, being compensatory to stance, gives her a wholeness that baffles definition in terms of any one thing and consequently seems nothing to those who must have certain belief and secure identity. Cordelia's and Prospero's nothingness and wholeness take the epistemic form of faith: a faith in human values for themselves that requires no reinforcement from beliefs about the universe and the gods. They are indifferent to security because their identity, being no thing, is not the object but the very source of their faith. Identity and the god-image, as Jung has shown, are interdependent; Cordelia and Prospero, by understanding their essential nothingness, transcend the struggle for secure ego identity and the need to project the self on external "gods."

A metastance to tragedy accords man transcendence of need for identity and divinity. Since his social, conscious, and real identities are bound in time, the fundamental truth beneath his identity is the inevitability of its loss and the loss of all he loves—dissolution to nothingness. Sensitivity to identity's ephemeral nature begets an impulse toward transcendence. The deficient transcendence that orthodox Christian theology displays in asserting as certain truths its fears and hopes for an afterlife in hell or heaven while reducing the existential fact of evil to *privatio boni* reveals a will to render time unreal, and with it evil and tragedy. Metastance, by achieving full transcendence, achieves acceptance of time, evil, and tragedy, and thus frees man from the need to believe them unreal and to believe in immortal ego identity and its surety, the gods. This feedom is a sine qua non for both faith and wholeness. The man who has conceived life as tragic can pass beyond Lear's final Promethean protest to a stage where neither awareness of tragedy nor need to deny its reality possesses him and the full self can be liberated.

Prospero speaks from the metastance of one who has transcended both tragedy and its denial to attain a vision of wholeness when he assures Ferdinand:

> You do look, my son, in a moved sort,
> As if you were dismay'd: be cheerful, sir.
> Our revels now are ended. These our actors
> As I foretold you, were all spirits and
> Are melted into air, into thin air:
> And, like the baseless fabric of this vision
> The cloud-capp'd towers, the gorgeous palaces,
> The solemn temples, the great globe itself,
> Yea, all which it inherit, shall dissolve
> And, like this insubstantial pageant faded,
> Leave not a rack behind. We are such stuff
> As dreams are made on, and our little life
> Is rounded in a sleep.
>
> (4.1.146–58)

Because Ferdinand has not achieved a metastance to change, time, and tragedy, he is easily dismayed at the dissolution of the pageant and distracted by grief at the loss of his father. But the pageant's disappearance provides Prospero with a simile to illumine the transience of man's life, the fragility of identity, and the universality of dissolution. As he moves from the dissolution of the masque to that of the actors in the play of life who will melt into sleep, Prospero teaches that art, the world, and identity are as ephemeral as the stuff of dreams.

In *The Tempest* man realizes transcendence in dissolution and subsequent transformation. When Ferdinand masters Prospero's instruction, he can accommodate dissolution and death and gain spiritual transformation and rebirth. Through rebirth a man becomes fully alive to his essential nothingness, and the conflicting stances that conscious identity assumes are superseded by the transcendent unity of metastance. After Ferdinand accepts the dissolution of his social identity as heir to Naples, he is ready to be reborn to a larger identity through marriage to Miranda, who symbolizes wisdom. Similarly, Prospero, sustained by Miranda, has adapted to the overthrow of his old identity as Duke of Milan and secured the higher identity of a Magus. Prospero's magic compensates for political power in the way that art compensates for morality, dreams for waking, madness for rationalism, love for indifference, metastance for stance, and self for ego. Magicians, artists, dreamers, madmen, and lovers all experience a dissolution of the stances ego identity takes, followed by a transformation that gives birth to a transcendent metastance opening upon the whole self.

Gonzalo's vision of Utopia, like Prospero's comments on the disappearance of the masque, illustrates creative dissolution. In his ideal commonwealth the political, social, and economic structures that generate social identity and inequality dissolve. This, he hopes, will restore ideal innocence and thus make possible a rebirth of the golden age:

> for no kind of traffic
> Would I admit; no name of magistrate;
> Letters should not be known; riches, poverty
> And the use of service, none; contract, succession,
> Bourn, bound of land, tilth, vinyard, none;
> No use of metal, corn, or wine, or oil;
> No occupation; all men idle, all;
> And women too, but innocent and pure;
> No sovereignty:
>
> (2.1.147–55)

Since the conscious identities of his auditors, the king, Antonio, and Sebastian, encompass no more than their conceptions of and attitudes toward social identity, Gonzalo's repudiation of social identity seems radical nonsense to them. The king declares, "Thou dost talk of nothing to me." The nothing Gonzalo talks about is man's real identity, which the king, like most political characters in Shakespeare, remains blind to. Gonzalo's arcadian "dream" about a place where social identity dissolves forms a revolutionary development of Lear's mad quest for social justice and Gloucester's call for redistributing wealth. Gonzalo well knows that social identity, because it fosters indurated personae that preclude self-knowledge and inhibit love and so alienate men from themselves and each other, necessarily encourages development of social injustice. From the histories to the last romances, Shakespeare stresses that to be true to himself and just to his fellows, an individual must experience the nothingness at the base of real identity by dissolving, or achieving a metastance to, social identity.

Antonio's retort to Gonzalo's assertion that the king's gentlemen always laugh at nothing, " 'Twas you we laughed at, " identifies the old lord with creative nothingness. Gonzalo affirms his own nothingness as he declares himself one "Who in this merry kind of fooling am nothing to you: / so you may continue to laugh at nothing still" (2.1.178–79). Gonzalo in his nothingness resembles the Fool and Cordelia, even as the treacherous Antonio and Sebastian resemble Goneril and Regan. Gonzalo, by knowing his nothingness has gained a metastance to social identity that shows him the irrelevance of old social values in the new world of the island. This makes him receptive to the island's magic. Antonio and Sebastian, who are alive only to the realities of social identity and political power, realities that have become phantasms on the strange island, try to impose their values on everything and remain blind to the magic around them. When their crimes are magically disclosed, they draw their swords in defiance. Although Antonio never repents any misdeeds, Prospero forgives him because he knows that his brother can no longer enjoy their fruits and wishes to purge all enmity from his own spirit. The contrast of Gonzalo to Antonio and Sebastian rests on the opposition of spontaneous goodness and receptive, flexible, conscious identity to incorrigible evil and rigid, hubristic, ego identity. It illustrates metastance's moral and spiritual superiority to unbending stance.

Magic dissolves the rigid social identities of all the characters thrown upon Prospero's enchanted shores. The magic of the storm strips from Alonso his identity as a king and from Ferdinand his identity as crown Prince. Antonio and Sebastian and Stephano and Trinculo, not realizing that the shipwreck has invalidated ordinary categories of social identity, try to seize the identities of Alonso and Prospero. Magic saves Alonso and Prospero from these would-be murderers, and magic effects Alonso's miraculous repentance, Prospero's restoration to his dukedom, and Ferdinand and Miranda's mutual acquisition of new identities in love. *The Tempest,* as Gonzalo exuberantly proclaims, concerns a magical voyage filled with wondrous discoveries:

> O, rejoice
> Beyond a common joy, and set it down
> With gold on lasting pillars: In one voyage
> Did Clairbel her husband find in Tunis
> And Ferdinand, her brother, found a wife
> Where he himself was lost, Prospero his dukedom
> In a poor isle and all of us ourselves
> When no man was his own.
>
> (5.1.206–13)

Magic is not only instrumental to resolving all the identity problems *The Tempest* sets forth; it also constitutes an essential facet of the metastance that underlies the play's meaning. Through transcendence, metastance can compensate for all one-sided conscious stances a person or culture takes. In the sixteenth and early seventeenth centuries Hermetic magic frequently formed a metastance to prevailing religious and scientific attitudes. Frances Yates's extensive studies of Renaissance Hermetic traditions provide concepts to illuminate both Prospero's role as magus and the play's metastance. The Hermetic movement, which at the time the play was written was being revived under the auspices of young Prince Henry, attempted to reform Christianity by replacing credulity with faith and dogmatism with tolerance. However, humanists and orthodox Christians, especially those sympathetic to Spain and Rome, deemed Hermetic magicians charlatans. Their bias appears in Ben Jonson's *The Alchemist*. Jonson's Subtle and Shakespeare's Prospero are the same archetypal figure viewed from opposite perspectives. Subtle constitutes a satiric portrait of the Magus that reinforces the cultural canon, and Prospero is a sympathetic portrait that vindicates the Hermetic tradition and the compensatory metastance it embodies.

Shakespeare, like the Hermetists, sees a dramatic artist in the magician and a magician in the dramatic artist. This similarity of dramatist and magician comes to light in Shakespeare's elaborate theatrical mechanisms— for example, those behind Prospero's masque and Jupiter's descent in *Cymbeline*—which resembled the technical operations Hermetic priests devised. To effect such operations Shakespeare may have used Hermetic techniques. If he did, they probably would not have seemed misplaced in the Globe; for the Globe (Yates hypothesizes) may well have been a magical "Theater of the World" constructed on Hermetic-Vitruvian principles. Concerning Prospero Yates writes:

> In Prospero we may now see, not only the Magus as philosopher and as all-powerful magician ushering in the scientific age about to dawn, but also the Magus as creator of the theater and its magic.
>
> *(Theatre of the World)*

Prospero, master of the spirits and master stage manipulator, is a perfect symbol for the magician-artist. His faith, tolerance, and willingness to forgive and strive for reform illustrate the best in Hermetic religious philosophy. Magic, art, and philosophy unite in Prospero to epitomize his creator's metastance to his time and culture, in which imaginative vision transcends the rigid, hubristic formulations of pedantry and dogmatism.

Jung's alchemical studies provide another perspective that can help us understand the symbolic import the Magus and his alchemy held. Metallic transformation, Jung contends, is metaphoric for self-transformation. Accordingly, in seeking the philosopher's stone, the greater alchemists were unconsciously questing for an inner transformation culminating in a rebirth to wholeness. Renaissance alchemists frequently identified the *lapis* with Christ; Christ, Jung asserts, symbolizes the self.

> Had the alchemist succeeded in forming any concrete idea of his unconscious contents, he would have been obliged to recognize that he had taken the place of Christ—or, to be more exact, that he, regarded not as ego but as self, had taken over the work of redeeming not man but God. He would then have had to recognize not only himself as the equivalent of Christ, but Christ as a symbol of the self.
>
> (*Psychology and Alchemy*)

I explained [elsewhere] that if we apply Jung's principle that the god-image is a function (i.e., a projection) of the self, we can perceive in *King Lear* a struggle to redeem God through actualizing the whole self. In *The Tempest* a great magician achieves the unconscious goal of both Lear and the alchemical quest. He controls the spirits, has power over matter, and redeems the self and God when he realizes the wholeness Cordelia symbolizes and Lear strives for.

Since he has purified himself to acquire the true gold of psychic wholeness, Prospero knows how to purify both Alonso and Ferdinand in an initiation process that gives them a metastance to their former identities that brings them closer to wholeness. Initiation involves a radical inner transformation by passion analogous to alchemy's transmutation of metals by fire. The old self, or unenlightened hubristic ego, which has been built on an indurated persona and reflects the social identity, dissolves, and a newly refined, conscious identity emerges that is sensitive to real identity and aspiring to ideal identity. Mircea Eliade traces the pattern that initiation rites follow:

> It is known that the essence of initiation into the Mysteries consisted of participation in the passion, death, and resurrection of a God. . . . The meaning and finality of the Mysteries were the transmutation of man. By experience of initiatory death and resurrection the initiate changed his mode of being (he became "immortal").
>
> (*The Forge and the Crucible*, trans. Stephen Corrin)

The passion, death, and resurrection that Eliade finds characterizing initiation are prefigured in Alonso's and Ferdinand's flight from their flame-engulfed ship, immersion in the sea, and safe arrival on Prospero's isle. Alonso enters the passional stage in the actual transmutation process with his loss of royal power and abasement and Ferdinand with his grief and "wooden slavery." Since "wood" meant mad, Alonso and Ferdinand's experiences form a comic parallel to Lear's humiliation and madness. The element fire calls to mind the alchemist's furnace and, obviously, represents passion's power to dissolve and transmute identity. Fire's importance is celebrated in the imagery in Ariel's description of his performance during the storm:

> I flamed amazement: sometime I'ld divide,
> And burn in many places; on the topmast,
> The yards and bowsprit, would I flame distinctly,
> Then meet and join. Jove's lightenings, the precursors
> O'th' dreadful thunder-claps, more momentary
> And sight out-running were not; the fire and cracks
> Of Sulphurous roaring.
>
> (1.2.198–204)

Among the royal party emerging from the sea, only Gonzalo retains the clarity of mind to appreciate the literal freshness of their drenched garments, for he alone needs no spiritual purification. His rancorous, guilty master, Alonso, on the other hand, needs total cleansing—a death or dissolution of hubristic ego:

> Full Fathom five thy father lies;
>   Of his bones are coral made;
> Those are pearls that were his eyes:
>   Nothing of him doth fade
> Both doth suffer a sea change
>   Into something new and strange.
>
> (1.2.396–401)

Before he can reunite with his son and regain monarchical identity, Alonso must suffer a purifying sea change of repentance. Similarly, before he can marry Miranda, Ferdinand must gain spiritual purification through accepting his father's death and the loss of his own social identity. *The Tempest*'s references to fire, wood, and grief, and water, death, and sleep suggest the purgatorial stages of initiation. Its references to dreams, waking, and miracles suggest the final stage—resurrection to a new identity. The alchemists, as Eliade indicates, strove to change their mode of being through mystical initiation. Prospero and his initiates Alonso and Ferdinand achieve such a change when they extend forgiveness, repent crime, and accept death. His magic tenders no promises for literal immortality, yet it can create a spiritual resurrection to a metastance of forgiveness, repentance, and acceptance that frees men from vindictiveness, guilt, and fear of death.

The initiatory rites awaken the soul. In *The Tempest* discovery of real identity and visions of ideal identity mark awakening. Alonso discovers his real identity; and, in Miranda, Ferdinand receives a vision of what the soul needs to attain wholeness. Miranda means wonder. Wonder forms the beginning of wisdom. Miranda symbolizes potential for the wisdom and truth that constitute the preliminary goals of the aspirant's quest for wholeness. The aspirant furthers love of wisdom in marriage to wonder. Since Miranda, like Cordelia, is a symbolic anima figure, we cannot expect her to represent realistically all the perfections attributed to her. But if we know that she symbolizes potential for the wisdom and truth that the aspirant must actualize to gain the wholeness of ideal identity, then Prospero's and Ferdinand's praise of her will not seem romantic silliness. Their enthusiasm, we shall realize, extends beyond Miranda herself to a vision of the final goal of human consciousness.

Throughout Miranda's young life Prospero has concealed their social identities from her. He calls her, "my daughter, who / Art ignorant of what thou art, not knowing / Of whence I am" (1.1.17–19). She observes:

> You have often
> Begun to tell me what I am, but stopp'd
> And left me to bootless inquisition,
> Concluding "Stay: not yet".
>
> (1.2.33–36)

Prospero does not discuss their lost social identity until the very day they are to regain it. Miranda's symbolic identity is, as one would expect, never so explicitly revealed as is her social identity. "Symbolic identity" refers to something numinous, which the social and real identities connote. Accordingly, because she is daughter to a great wiseman and since wisdom, in the biblical tradition, comes from the mouths of babes, Miranda's parentage and innocence make her an appropriate symbol for potential wisdom. Though she in her ignorance of evil cannot fully possess wisdom, her patience, purity, sense of wonder, and truthfulness are all necessary conditions for attaining wisdom.

As *The Tempest* unfolds Prospero and Miranda regain lost social identity, and Miranda, Alonso, and Ferdinand reach a clearer understanding of their real identities and move toward the ideal identity that Prospero and, to a lesser extent, Gonzalo embody. Antonio, Sebastian, Stephano, and Trinculo, by contrast, try to steal new social identities. All of these characters also have some degree of symbolic identity. The identities Caliban and Ariel assume, however, are almost exclusively symbolical, and the terms *social, real,* and *ideal* identity seem scarcely applicable to them. Caliban represents earthly matter and is associated with water; Ariel represents air, spirit, and fire. Caliban also exemplifies the radical, incorrigible evil of which Antonio provides a realistic representation. He is, Prospero declares, "a born devil, on whose nature nurture can never stick." When he tempts Stephano, Caliban plays the devil—a role he shares with Sebastian's tempter, Antonio. Because he has no power, Caliban remains a comic devil. His piscatory appearance makes him a ludicrous parody of Jung's second fish, which in its tragic form is identified with Leviathan and is analogous to Goneril. (Jung discusses the two fishes that were the alchemical symbols for Christ and Satan. We can only conjecture whether Shakespeare had the alchemical second fish in mind when he created his "plain fish," the "born devil" Caliban.) The second fish and Caliban embody the irrational, unteachable malice that brute nature displays.

Ariel is a more complex figure. His symbolic identity, like that of his master, Prospero, takes its roots deep in the alchemical tradition. Ariel so resembles Mercury, especially the alchemist's Mercury, that this parallel must have been fully conscious (indeed he contrasts to the beleaguered sprite in Jonson's satiric masque *Mercury Vindicated from the Alchemists* in similar manner to the contrast of Prospero and Subtle). Like Mercury, he is a messenger, swift, quick-witted, fickle, many-sided, fiery, and he lives in the air. Jung notes that the alchemical treatises often define Mercury simply as fire. The alchemists, he adds, universally regarded Mercury as their God and labored to subject him and his fiery powers to their control. The aspirant magician, the treatises maintain, can find Mercury incarcerated in a tree or a bottle. When he secures hegemony over Ariel-Mercury by releasing him from the tree where Sycorax has confined him, Prospero establishes his identity as a very powerful magician—indeed, the archetypal magician. Prospero underlines Ariel's mercurial nature with the charge that he is moody and with the epithet *tricksy spirit*. Ariel reveals his deficient moral sense in an admission that he feels no compassion. Jung contends that Mercury's unpredictable and amoral character makes him a quasi-devilish being. The magician's struggle to master Mercury, who, like Satan, acts to offset the orthodox Christ, symbolizes a quest for rule over man's darker side, the shadow, as well as for rule of nature. Prospero's dominion over Ariel epitomizes command of his own nonmoral, mercurial side, a command most evident in choosing "the rarer action."

The Tempest begins with an impressive display of those powers which mastery of Ariel gives Prospero. Prospero's powers, however, are not without limitations. And he knows these limitations well, for his studies have given him the means to apprehend Fortune's course:

and by my prescience
I find my zenith doth depend upon
A most auspicious star, whose influence
If I now court not but omit, my fortunes
Will ever after droop.

(1.2.180–84)

Astrology was doubtless among the secret studies with which Prospero was rapt and transported prior to Antonio's treachery. The greatest astrologer cannot vanquish time, but, through understanding time, he can find the most auspicious moment for every act. Timing for the astrologer-magician, as for the dramatist and the statesman, proves all-important. Timing allows each a limited freedom within the confines his art imposes. Prospero secures such a freedom when he recognizes the necessity to exploit opportunities the moment they occur.

However, he achieves freedom in its highest manifestation—wholeness—through accepting man's uttermost limit, ineluctable death. After he frees Ariel and abdicates the magician's role to resume that of Duke of Milan, Prospero declares that in Milan every third thought shall be his grave. We give Prospero's vow too literal an interpretation if we deem it evidence that he has entered advanced age and expects to die soon. It means only that, since he has regained the Dukedom and both defeated and accepted human and natural evil, he is now fully prepared for death. He has the ultimate freedom signified by the wise old man archetype, a serene awareness of tragedy, time, evil, and death. Such freedom is neither old age's inevitable fruit, as Lear so painfully demonstrates, nor is it, as the maturing Hamlet illustrates, entirely denied the young. It comes to any who can attain metastance.

Prospero's power began with mastering Ariel and Caliban, but consummation of freedom waits upon their liberation. A man is truly free if no part of the self needs to be imprisoned or repressed. To the extent that Ariel and Caliban are projections from Prospero's penumbral self or shadow, their liberation advances his search for inner freedom. The moment Prospero forgives Caliban and acknowledges him his own, he accepts his own darkest, most primitive side. The moment he frees Ariel, he frees himself from reliance on unintegrated powers and establishes the full spiritual harmony and self-dependence that wholeness bestows. With these two acts the Magus archetype encompasses the wise old man archetype, and the quest for wholeness has entered its final stage of quiet waiting for death.

Lear shows how fear of death spurs the drive for arbitrary power. Prospero dramatizes preparedness for death as he breaks his staff and symbolically renounces power for faith. He again becomes physically vulnerable to Antonio's evil, but for this loss he gains true spiritual freedom. The man who relies on power to guarantee him security and certainty becomes enslaved to that power. Man's flight from faith is a flight from freedom driven by fear of identity loss and death. If we view Prospero as a successor to Lear, we can see in Shakespeare's last romance man's transcending the need for identity secured with power to find identity sustained through faith. Prospero has used his magic arts to influence the spirits or gods and thus gain the power Lear so vainly sought in prayers and curses:

> to the dread rattling thunder
> Have I given fire and rifted Jove's stout oak
> With his own bolt; the strong based promontory
> Have I made to shake and by the spurs pluck'd up
> The pine and cedar: graves at my command
> Have wak'd their sleepers, op'd, and let 'em forth
> By my so potent Art. But this rough magic
> I here abjure.
>
> (5.1.41–48)

The spirits do not ignore Prospero. Yet he chooses to abjure power over them because he knows that he must free them in order to perfect inner freedom and attain wholeness. Faith proves to be finally the most potent magic. Faith's alchemy forms a metastance wherein fears of identity loss through death, evil, and tragedy are dispelled, need for secure identity is transcended, and dependence, hubristic egoism, despair, and dogmatism are all displaced. Those who labor to maintain secure identity by confining parts of their spirit are not free, but enslaved to identity.

The spirit of the archetypal poet, like that of the archetypal magician and seer, gains its freedom once he reaches a metastance to his own identity—if you will, a meta-identity. As Keats put is, the ideal poet is a creator of identities who himself has no identity. His metastance makes him an open window to both soul and cosmos. In *The Tempest* the poet's metastance discloses a dissolution of rigid ego identity that intimates a unity of being wherein, to borrow Northrop Frye's words, "there is only one man, one mind, one world, and all the walls of partition have been broken down for ever." By transcending the bounds identity imposes through a metastance of ego-free consciousness, the archetypal poet, magician, and seer attain a vision compensatory to the tragic fragmentation of ordinary life, a comedic vision of the self and the universe in which both are whole.

Prospero's Wife

Stephen Orgel

This essay is not a reading of *The Tempest*. It is a consideration of five related moments and issues. I have called it "Prospero's Wife" because some of it centers on her, but in a larger sense because she is a figure conspicuous by her absence from the play, and my large subject is the absent, the unspoken, that seems to me the most powerful and problematic presence in *The Tempest*. In its outlines, the play seems a story of privatives: withdrawal, usurpation, banishment, the loss of one's way, shipwreck. As an antithesis, a principle of control, preservation, re-creation, the play offers only magic, embodied in a single figure, the extraordinary powers of Prospero.

Prospero's wife is alluded to only once in the play, in Prospero's reply to Miranda's question. "Sir, are you not my father?"

> Thy mother was a piece of virtue, and
> She said thou wast my daughter; and thy father
> Was Duke of Milan; and his only heir
> And princess: no worse issued.
>
> (1.2.55–59)

Prospero's wife is identified as Miranda's mother, in a context implying that though she was virtuous, women as a class are not, and that were it not for her word, Miranda's legitimacy would be in doubt. The legitimacy of Prospero's heir, that is, derives from her mother's word. But that word

From *Representations* 8 (Fall 1984). © 1984 by the Regents of the University of California.

is all that is required of her in the play. Once he is assured of it, Prospero turns his attention to himself and his succession, and he characterizes Miranda in a clause that grows increasingly ambivalent—"his only heir / And princess: no worse issued."

Except for this moment, Prospero's wife is absent from his memory. She is wholly absent from her daughter's memory: Miranda can recall several women who attended her in childhood, but no mother. The implied attitudes toward wives and mothers here are confirmed shortly afterward when Prospero, recounting his brother Antonio's crimes, demands that Miranda "tell me / If this might be a brother," and Miranda takes the question to be a charge of adultery against Prospero's mother:

> I should sin
> To think but nobly of my grandmother:
> Good wombs have borne bad sons.
> (1.2.118–20)

She immediately translates Prospero's attack on his brother into an attack on his mother (the best she can produce in her grandmother's defence is a "not proved"), and whether or not she has correctly divined her father's intentions, Prospero makes no objection.

The absent presence of the wife and mother in the play constitutes a space that is filled by Prospero's creation of surrogates and a ghostly family: the witch Sycorax and her monster child, Caliban (himself, as becomes apparent, a surrogate for the other wicked child, the usurping younger brother), the good child/wife Miranda, the obedient Ariel, the violently libidinized adolescent Ferdinand. The space is filled, too, by a whole structure of wifely allusion and reference: widow Dido, model at once of heroic fidelity to a murdered husband and the destructive potential of erotic passion; the witch Medea, murderess and filicide; three exemplary goddesses, the bereft Ceres, nurturing Juno and licentious Venus; and Alonso's daughter, Claribel, unwillingly married off to the ruler of the modern Carthage, and thereby lost to her father forever.

Described in this way, the play has an obvious psychoanalytic shape. I have learned a great deal from Freudian treatments of it, most recently from essays by David Sundelson, Coppélia Kahn and Joel Fineman in the volume called *Representing Shakespeare*. It is almost irresistible to look at the play as a case history. *Whose* case history is a rather more problematic question, and one that criticism has not, on the whole, dealt with satisfactorily. It is not, obviously, that of the characters. I want to pause first over what it means to consider the play as a case history.

In older psychoanalytic paradigms (say Ernest Jones's) the critic is the analyst, Shakespeare is the patient, the plays his fantasies. The trouble with this paradigm is that it misrepresents the analytic situation in a fundamental way. The interpretation of analytic material is done in conjunction with, and in large measure by, the patient, not the analyst; what the analyst does is *enable* the patient, free the patient to interpret. An analysis done without the patient, like Freud's of Leonardo, will be revealing only about the analyst. A more recent paradigm, in which the audience's response is the principal analytic material, also seems to me based on fundamental misconceptions, first because it treats an audience as an entity, a unit, and in addition a constant one, and more problematically, because it conceives of the play as an objective event, so that the critical question becomes, "this is what happened: how do we respond to it?"

To take the psychoanalytic paradigm seriously, however, and treat the plays as case histories, is surely to treat them *not* as objective events but as collaborative fantasies, and to acknowledge thereby that we, as analysts, are implicated in the fantasy. It is not only the patient who creates the shape of his history, and when Bruno Bettelheim observes that Freud's case histories "read as well as the best novels," he is probably telling more of the truth than he intends. Moreover, the crucial recent advances in our understanding of Freud and psychoanalysis have been precisely critical acts of close and inventive reading—there are, in this respect, no limits to the collaboration. But if we accept this as our paradigm, and think of ourselves as Freud's or Shakespeare's collaborators, we must also acknowledge that our reading of the case will be revealing, again, chiefly about ourselves. This is why every generation, and perhaps every reading, produces a different analysis of its Shakespearean texts. In the same way, recent psychoanalytic theory has replaced Freud's central Oedipal myth with a drama in which the loss of the seducing mother is the crucial infant trauma. We used to want assurance that we would successfully compete with or replace or supersede our fathers; now we want to know that our lost mothers will return. Both of these no doubt involve real perceptions, but they also undeniably serve particular cultural needs.

Shakespeare plays, like case histories, derive from the observation of human behavior, and both plays and case histories are imaginative constructs. Whether either is taken to be an objective report of behavior or not has more to do with the reader than the reporter, but it has to be said that Shakespearean critics have more often than not treated the plays as objective accounts. Without such an assumption, a book with the title *The Girlhood of Shakespeare's Heroines* would be incomprehensible. We feel very far from this famous and popular Victorian work now, but we still worry about consistency and motivation in Shakespearean texts, and much of the commentary in an edition like the Arden Shakespeare is designed to explain why the characters say what they say—that is, to reconcile what they say with what, on the basis of their previous behavior, we feel they ought to be saying. The critic who worries about this kind of consistency in a Shakespeare text is thinking of it as an objective report.

But all readings of Shakespeare, from the earliest seventeenth-century adaptations, through eighteenth-century attempts to produce "authentic" or "accurate" texts, to the liberal fantasy of the old Variorum Shakespeare, have been aware of deep ambiguities and ambivalences in the texts. The eighteenth century described these as Shakespeare's errors, and generally revised them through plausible emendation or outright rewriting. The argument was that Shakespeare wrote in haste, and would have written more perfect plays had he taken time to revise; the corollary to this was, of course, that what we want are the perfect plays Shakespeare did not write, rather than the imperfect ones that he did. A little later the errors became not Shakespeare's but those of the printing house, the scribe, the memory of the reporter or the defective hearing of the transcriber. But the assumption has always been that it is possible to produce a "perfect" text: that beyond or behind the ambiguous, puzzling, inconsistent text is a clear and consistent one.

Plays, moreover, are not only—and one might argue, not primarily—texts. They are performances too, originally designed to be read only in order to be acted out, and the gap between the text and its performance has always been, and remains, a radical one. There always has been an imagination intervening between the texts and their audiences, initially the imagination of producer, director, actor (roles that Shakespeare played himself), and since that time the imagination of editors and commentators as well. These are texts that have always had to be *realized*. Initially unstable, they have remained so despite all our attempts to fix them. All our attempts to produce an authentic, correct, that is, *stable* text have resulted only in an extraordinary variety of versions. Their differences can be described as minor only if one believes that the real play is a Platonic idea, never realized but only approached and approximately represented by its text.

This is our myth: the myth of a stable, accurate, authentic, *legitimate* text, a text that we can think of as Shakespeare's legitimate heir. It is, in its way, a genealogical myth, and it operates with peculiar force in our readings of *The Tempest,* a play that has been, for the last hundred and fifty years, taken as a representation of Shakespeare himself bidding farewell to his art—as Shakespeare's legacy.

THE MISSING WIFE

She is missing as a character, but Prospero, several times explicitly, presents himself as incorporating her, acting as both father and mother to Miranda, and in one extraordinary passage describes the voyage to the island as a birth fantasy:

> When I have decked the sea with drops full salt,
> Under my burden groaned, which raised in me
> An undergoing stomach, to bear up
> Against what should ensue.
>
> (1.2.155–58)

To come to the island is to start life over again—both his own and Miranda's—with himself as sole parent, but also with himself as favorite child. He has been banished by his wicked, usurping, possibly illegitimate younger brother Antonio. This too has the shape of a Freudian fantasy: the younger child *is* the usurper in the family, and the kingdom he usurps is the mother. On the island, Prospero undoes the usurpation, re-creating kingdom and family with himself in sole command.

But not quite, because the island is not his alone. Or if it is, then he has repeopled it with all parts of his fantasy, the distressing as well as the gratifying. When he arrives he finds Caliban, child of the witch Sycorax, herself a victim of banishment. The island provided a new life for her too, as it did literally for her son, with whom she was pregnant when she arrived. Sycorax died some time before Prospero came to the island; Prospero never saw her, and everything he knows about her he has learned from Ariel. Nevertheless, she is insistently present in his memory—far more present than his own wife—and she embodies to an extreme degree all the negative assumptions about women that he and Miranda have exchanged.

It is important, therefore, that Caliban derives his claim to the island from his mother: "This island's mine, by Sycorax my mother" (1.2.333). This has interesting implications to which I shall return, but here I want to point out that he need not make the claim this way. He could derive it from the mere fact of prior possession: he was there first. This, after all, would have been the sole basis of Sycorax's claim to the island, but it is an argument that Caliban never makes. And in deriving his authority from his mother, he delivers himself into Prospero's hands. Prospero declares him a bastard, "got by the devil himself / Upon thy wicked dam" (1.2.321–22), thereby both disallowing any claim from inheritance and justifying his loathing for Caliban.

But is it true that Caliban is Sycorax's bastard by Satan? How does

Prospero know this? Not from Sycorax: Prospero never saw her. Not from Caliban: Sycorax died before she could even teach her son to speak. Everything Prospero knows about the witch he knows from Ariel—her appearance, the story of her banishment, the fact that her pregnancy saved her from execution. Did Sycorax also tell Ariel that her baby was the illegitimate son of the devil? Or is this Prospero's contribution to the story, an especially creative piece of invective, and an extreme instance of his characteristic assumptions about women? Nothing in the text will answer this question for us, and it is worth pausing to observe first that Caliban's claim seems to have been designed so that Prospero can disallow it, and second that we have no way of distinguishing the facts about Caliban and Sycorax from Prospero's invective about them.

Can Prospero imagine no good mothers, then? The play, after all, moves toward a wedding, and the most palpable example we see of the magician's powers is a betrothal masque. The masque is presided over by two exemplary mothers, Ceres and Juno, and the libidinous Venus with her destructive son Cupid has been banished from the scene. But the performance is also preceded by the most awful warnings against sexuality—male sexuality this time: all the libido is presumed to be Ferdinand's, while Miranda remains Prospero's innocent child. Ferdinand's reassuring reply, as David Sundelson persuasively argues, includes submerged fantasies of rape and more than a hint that when the lust of the wedding night cools, so will his marital devotion:

> the murkiest den,
> The most opportune place, the strong'st suggestion
> Our worser genius can, shall never melt
> Mine honor into lust, to take away
> The edge of that day's celebration.
>
> (4.1.25–29)

This is the other side of the assumption that all women at heart are whores: all men at heart are rapists—Caliban, Ferdinand, and of course that means Prospero too.

THE MARRIAGE CONTRACT

The play moves toward marriage, certainly, yet the relations it postulates between men and women are ignorant at best, characteristically tense, and potentially tragic. There is a familiar Shakespearean paradigm here: relationships between men and women interest Shakespeare intensely, but not, on the whole, as husbands and wives. The wooing process tends to be what it is here: not so much a prelude to marriage and a family as a process of self-definition—an increasingly unsatisfactory process, if we look at the progression of plays from *As You Like It, Much Ado about Nothing, Twelfth Night* through *All's Well That Ends Well, Measure for Measure, Troilus and Cressida* to *Antony and Cleopatra* and *Cymbeline*. If we want to argue that marriage *is* the point of the comic wooing process for Shakespeare, then we surely ought to be looking at how he depicts marriages. Here Petruchio and Kate, Capulet and Lady Capulet, Claudius and Gertrude, Othello and Desdemona, Macbeth and Lady Macbeth, Cymbeline and his queen, Leontes and Hermione will not persuade us that comedies ending in marriages have ended happily, or if they have, it is only because they have ended there, stopped at the wedding day.

What happens after marriage? Families in Shakespeare tend to consist not of husbands and wives and their offspring, but of a parent and a child, usually in a chiastic relationship: father and daughter, mother and son. When there are two children, they tend to be represented as alternatives or rivals: the twins of *The Comedy of Errors,* Sebastian and Viola, infinitely substitutable for each other, or the good son-bad son complex of Orlando and Oliver, Edgar and Edmund. We know that Shakespeare himself had a son and two daughters, but that family configuration never appears in the plays. Lear's three daughters are quite exceptional in Shakespeare, and even they are dichotomized into bad and good. We might also recall Titus Andronicus's four sons and a daughter and Tamora's three sons, hardly instances to demonstrate Shakespeare's convictions about the comforts of family life.

The family paradigm that emerges from Shakespeare's imagination is a distinctly unstable one. Here is what we know of Shakespeare's own family: he had three brothers and three sisters who survived beyond infancy, and his parents lived into old age. At eighteen he married a woman of twenty-four by whom he had a daughter within six months, and a twin son and daughter a year and a half later. Within six more years he had moved permanently to London, and for the next twenty years—all but the last three years of his life—he lived apart from his wife and family. Nor should we stop here: we do not in the least know that Susanna, Hamnet, and Judith were his only children. He lived in a society without contraceptives, and unless we want to believe that he was either exclusively homosexual or celibate, we must assume a high degree of probability that there were other children. The fact that they are not mentioned in his will may mean that they did not survive, but it also might mean that he made separate, non-testamentary provision for them. Certainly the plays reveal a strong interest in the subject of illegitimacy.

Until quite late in his career, the strongest familial feelings seem to be expressed not toward children or wives but toward parents and siblings.

His father dies in 1601, the year of *Hamlet,* his mother in 1608, the year of *Coriolanus.* And if we are thinking about usurping, bastard younger brothers, it cannot be coincidental that the younger brother who followed him into the acting profession was named Edmund. There are no dramatic correlatives comparable to these for the death of his son Hamnet in 1596. If we take the plays to express what Shakespeare thought about himself (I put it that way to indicate that the assumption strikes me as by no means axiomatic) then we will say that he was apparently free to think of himself as a father—to his two surviving daughters—only after the death of both his parents. The year 1608 is the date of *Pericles* as well as *Coriolanus.*

One final biographical observation: Shakespearean heroines marry very young, in their teens. Miranda is fifteen. We are always told that Juliet's marriage at fourteen is not unusual in the period, but in fact it *is* unusual in all but upper-class families. In Shakespeare's own family, his wife married at twenty-four and his daughters at twenty-four and thirty-one. It was Shakespeare himself who married at eighteen. The women of Shakespeare's plays, of course, are adolescent boys. Perhaps we should see as much of Shakespeare in Miranda and Ariel as in Prospero.

Power and Authority

The psychoanalytic and biographical questions raised by *The Tempest* are irresistible, but they can supply at best partial clues to its nature. I have described the plays as collaborative fantasies, and it is not only critics and readers who are involved in the collaboration. It is performers and audiences too, and I take these terms in their largest senses, to apply not merely to stage productions, but to the theatrical dimension of the society that contains and is mirrored by the theater as well. Cultural concerns, political and social issues, speak through *The Tempest*—sometimes explicitly, as in the open-ended discussion of political economy between Gonzalo, Antonio, and Sebastian in act 2. But in a broader sense, family structures and sexual relations become political structures in the play, and these are relevant to the political structures of Jacobean England.

What is the nature of Prospero's authority and the source of his power? Why is he Duke of Milan and the legitimate ruler of the island? Power, as Prospero presents it in the play, is not inherited but self-created. It is magic, or "art," an extension of mental power and self-knowledge, and the authority legitimizing it derives from heaven—"Fortune" and "Destiny" are the terms used in the play. It is *Caliban* who derives his claim to the island from inheritance, from his mother.

In the England of 1610, both these positions represent available, and indeed normative ways of conceiving of royal authority. James I's authority derived, he said, both from his mother and from God. But deriving one's legitimacy from Mary Queen of Scots was an ambiguous claim at best, and James always felt exceedingly insecure about it. Elizabeth had had similar problems with the sources of her own authority, and they centered precisely on the question of her legitimacy. To those who believed that her father's divorce from Katherine of Aragon was invalid (that is, to Catholics), Elizabeth had no hereditary claim; and she had, moreover, been declared legally illegitimate after the execution of her mother for adultery and incest. Henry VIII maintained Elizabeth's bastardy to the end. Her claim to the throne derived exclusively from her designation in the line of succession, next after Edward and Mary, in her father's will. This ambiguous legacy was the sole source of her authority. Prospero at last acknowledging the bastard Caliban as his own is also expressing the double edge of kingship throughout Shakespeare's lifetime (the ambivalence will not surprise us if we consider the way kings are represented in the history plays). Historically speaking, Caliban's claim to the island is a good one.

Royal power, the play seems to say, is good when it is self-created, bad when it is usurped or inherited from an evil mother. But of course the least problematic case of royal descent is one that is not represented in these paradigms at all, one that derives not from the mother but in the male line from the father: the case of Ferdinand and Alonso, in which the wife and mother is totally absent. If we are thinking about the *derivation* of royal authority, then, the absence of a father from Prospero's memory is a great deal more significant than the disappearance of a wife. This has been dealt with in psychoanalytic terms, whereby Antonio becomes a stand-in for the father, the real usurper of the mother's kingdom; but here again the realities of contemporary kingship seem more enlightening, if not inescapable. James in fact had a double claim to the English throne, and the one through his father, the Earl of Darnley, was in the strictly lineal respects somewhat stronger than that of his mother. Both Darnley and Mary were direct descendants of Henry VII, but under Henry VIII's will, which established the line of succession, descendants who were not English-born were specifically excluded. Darnley was born in England, Mary was not. In fact, Darnley's mother went from Scotland to have her baby in England precisely in order to preserve the claim to the throne.

King James rarely mentioned this side of his heritage, for perfectly understandable reasons. His father was even more disreputable than his mother; and given what was at least the public perception of both their characters, it was all to easy to speculate about whether Darnley was even in fact his father. For James, as for Elizabeth, the derivation of authority through paternity was extremely problematic. In practical terms, James's claim to the English throne depended on Elizabeth *naming* him her heir (we recall Miranda's legitimacy depending on her mother's word), and James correctly saw this as a continuation of the protracted negotiations between Elizabeth and his mother. His legitimacy, in both senses, thus derived from two mothers, the chaste Elizabeth and the sensual Mary, whom popular imagery represented respectively as a virgin goddess ("a piece of virtue") and a lustful and diabolical witch. James's sense of his own place in the kingdom is that of Prospero, rigidly paternalistic, but incorporating the maternal as well: the King describes himself in *Basilicon Doron* as "a loving nourish father" providing the commonwealth with "their own nourish-milk." The very etymology of the word "authority" confirms the metaphor: *augeo*, "increase, nourish, cause to grow." At moments in his public utterances, James sounds like a gloss on Prospero: "I am the husband, and the whole island is my lawful wife; I am the head, and it is my body." Here the incorporation of the wife has become literal and explicit. James conceives himself as the head of a single-parent family. In the world of *The Tempest,* there are no two-parent families. All the dangers of promiscuity and bastardy are resolved in such a conception—unless, of course, the parent is a woman.

My point here is not that Shakespeare is representing King James as Prospero and/or Caliban, but that these figures embody the predominant modes of conceiving of royal authority in the period. They are Elizabeth's and James's modes too.

The Renunciation of Magic

Prospero's magic power is exemplified, on the whole, as power over children: his daughter Miranda, the bad child Caliban, the obedient but impatient Ariel, the adolescent Ferdinand, the wicked younger brother Antonio, and indeed, the shipwreck victims as a whole, who are treated like a group of bad children. Many critics talk about Prospero as a Renaissance scientist, and see alchemical metaphors in the grand design of the play. No doubt there is something in this, but what the play's action presents is not experiments and empiric studies but a fantasy about controlling other people's minds. Does the magic work? We are given a good deal of evidence of it: the masque, the banquet, the harpies, the tempest itself. But the great scheme is not to produce illusions and good weather, it is to bring about reconciliation, and here we would have to say that it works only indifferently well. "They being penitent," says Prospero to Ariel, "The sole drift of my purpose doth extend / Not a frown further" (5.1.28–30). The assertion opens with a conditional clause whose conditions are not met: Alonso is penitent, but the chief villain, the usurping younger brother Antonio, remains obdurate. Nothing, not all Prospero's magic, can redeem Antonio from his essential badness. Since Shakespeare was free to have Antonio repent if that is what he had in mind—half a line would have done for critics craving a reconciliation—we ought to take seriously the possibility that that is not what he had in mind. Perhaps, too, penitence is not what Prospero's magic is designed to elicit from his brother.

Why is Prospero's power conceived as magic? Why, in returning to Milan, does he renounce it? Most commentators say that he gives up his magic when he no longer needs it. This is an obvious answer, but it strikes me as too easy, a comfortable assumption cognate with the view that the play concludes with reconciliation, repentance, and restored harmony. To say that Prospero no longer *needs* his magic is to beg all the most important questions. What does it mean to say that he needs it? Did he ever need it, and if so, why? And does he in fact give it up?

Did he ever need magic? Prospero's devotion to his secret studies is what caused all the trouble in the first place—this is not an interpretation of mine, it is how Prospero presents the matter. If he has now learned to be a good ruler through the exercise of his art, that is also what taught him to be a bad one. So the question of his *need* for magic goes to the heart of how we interpret and judge his character: is the magic a strength or a weakness? To say that he no longer needs it is to say that his character changes in some way for the better, that by renouncing his special powers he becomes fully human. This is an important claim: let us test it by looking at Prospero's renunciation.

What does it mean for Prospero to give up his power? Letting Miranda marry and leaving the island are the obvious answers, but they can hardly be right. Miranda's marriage is *brought about* by the magic; it is part of Prospero's plan. It pleases Miranda, certainly, but it is designed by Prospero as a way of satisfying himself. Claribel's marriage to the King of Tunis looks less sinister in this light: daughters' marriages, in royal families at least, are designed primarily to please their fathers. And leaving the island, reassuming the dukedom, is part of the plan too. Both of these are presented as acts of renunciation, but they are in fact what the exercise of Prospero's magic is intended to effect, and they represent his triumph.

Prospero renounces his art in the great monologue at the beginning of act 5. "Ye elves of hills, brooks, standing lakes and groves," and for all its valedictory quality, it is the most powerful assertion of his magic the play gives us. It is also a powerful literary allusion, a close translation of a speech of Medea's in Ovid (*Metamorphoses* 7.197–209, apparently at least partly refracted through Golding's English version), and it makes at least one claim for Prospero that is made nowhere else in the play: that he can raise the dead. For Shakespeare to present this as a *renunciation* speech is upping Prospero's ante, to say the least.

In giving up his magic, Prospero speaks as Medea. He has incorporated Ovid's witch, prototype of the wicked mother Sycorax, in the most literal way—verbatim, so to speak—and his "most potent art" is now revealed as translation and impersonation. In this context, the distinction between black and white magic, Sycorax and Prospero, has disappeared. Two hundred lines later, Caliban too is revealed as an aspect of Prospero: "This thing of darkness I acknowledge mine."

But Caliban is an aspect of Antonio, the evil child, the usurping brother. Where is the *real* villain in relation to Prospero now? Initially Antonio had been characterized, like Caliban and Sycorax, as embodying everything that is antithetical to Prospero. But in recounting his history to Miranda, Prospero also presents himself as deeply implicated in the usurpation, with Antonio even seeming at times to be acting as Prospero's agent: "The government I cast upon my brother"; "[I] to him put the manage of my state"; "my trust . . . did beget of him / A falsehood," and so forth. If Prospero is accepting the blame for what happened, there is a degree to which he is also taking the credit. Antonio's is another of the play's identities that Prospero has incorporated into his own, and in that case, what is there to forgive?

Let us look, then, at Prospero forgiving his brother in act 5. The pardon is enunciated ("You, brother mine, that entertain ambition. . . . I do forgive thee" [ll. 75–78, Kermode and most editors read "entertained," but I have restored the folio reading, which seems to me unexceptionable]) and qualified at once ("unnatural though thou art"), reconsidered as more crimes are remembered, some to be held in reserve ("at this time I will tell no tales" [ll. 128–29]), all but withdrawn ("most wicked sir, whom to call brother / Would even infect my mouth" [ll. 130–31]), and only then confirmed through forcing Antonio to relinquish the dukedom, an act that is presented as something he does unwillingly. The point is not only that Antonio does not repent here: he also is not *allowed* to repent. Even his renunciation of the crown is Prospero's act: "I do . . . require / My dukedom of thee, which perforce, I know, / Thou must restore" (ll. 131–34). In Prospero's drama, there is no room for Antonio to act of his own free will.

The crime that Prospero holds in reserve for later use against his brother is the attempted assassination of Alonso. Here is what happened. Prospero sends Ariel to put all the shipwreck victims to sleep except Antonio and Sebastian. Antonio then persuades Sebastian to murder Alonso—his brother—and thereby become King of Naples. Sebastian agrees, on the condition that Antonio kill Gonzalo. At the moment of the murders, Ariel reappears and wakes Gonzalo:

> My master through his art foresees the danger
> That you his friend are in; and sends me forth—
> For else his project dies—to keep them living.
> (2.1.293–95)

This situation has been created by Prospero, and the conspiracy is certainly part of his project—that is why Sebastian and Antonio are not put to sleep. If Antonio is not forced by Prospero to propose the murder, he is certainly acting as Prospero expects him to do, and as Ariel says, Prospero "through his art foresees" that he will. What is clearly taking place is Prospero restaging his usurpation and maintaining his control over it this time. Gonzalo is waked rather than Alonso so that the old courtier can replay his role in aborting the assassination.

So at the play's end, Prospero still has usurpation and attempted murder to hold against his brother, things that still disqualify Antonio from his place in the family. Obviously there is more to Prospero's plans than reconciliation and harmony—even, I would think, in the forthcoming happy marriage of Ferdinand and Miranda. If we look at that marriage as a political act (the participants are, after all, the children of monarchs) we will observe that in order to prevent the succession of his brother, Prospero is marrying his daughter to the son of his enemy. This has the effect of excluding Antonio from any future claim on the ducal throne, but it also effectively disposes of the realm as a political entity: if Miranda is the heir to the dukedom, Milan through the marriage becomes part of the kingdom of Naples, not the other way around. Prospero recoups his throne from his brother only to deliver it over, upon his death, to the King of Naples once again. The usurping Antonio stands condemned, but the effects of the usurpation, the link with Alonso and the reduction of Milan to a Neapolitan fiefdom are, through Miranda's wedding, confirmed and legitimized. Prospero has not regained his lost dukedom, he has usurped his brother's. In this context, Prospero's puzzling assertion that "every third thought shall be my grave" can be seen as a final assertion of authority and control: he has now arranged matters so that his death will remove Antonio's last link with the ducal power. His grave is the ultimate triumph over his brother.

If we look at the marriage in this way, giving away Miranda is a means of preserving his authority, not of relinquishing it.

A BIBLIOGRAPHICAL CODA

The significant absence of crucial wives from the play is curiously emphasized by a famous textual crux. In act 4 Ferdinand, overwhelmed by the beauty of the masque Prospero is presenting, interrupts the performance to say,

> Let me live here, ever.
> So rare a wondered father and a wise
> Makes this place Paradise.
>
> (4.1.122–24)

Critics since the eighteenth century have expressed a nagging worry about the fact that in celebrating his betrothal, Ferdinand's paradise includes Prospero but not Miranda. In fact, what Ferdinand said, as Jeanne Addison Roberts demonstrated [several] years ago, reads in the earliest copies of the folio, "So rare a wondered father and a *wife*," but the crossbar of the *f* broke early in the print run, turning it to a long *s* and thereby eliminating Miranda from Ferdinand's thoughts of wonder. The odd thing about this is that Rowe and Malone in their eighteenth-century editions emended "wise" to "wife" on logical grounds, the Cambridge Shakespeare of 1863 lists "wife" as a variant reading of the folio, and Furnivall's 1895 photographic facsimile was made from a copy that reads "wife," and the reading is preserved in Furnivall's parallel text. Nevertheless, after 1895 the wife became invisible: bibliographers lost the variant, and textual critics consistently denied its existence until six years ago. Even Charlton Hinman with his collating machines claimed there were no variants whatever in this entire forme of the folio. And yet when Jeanne Roberts examined the Folger Library's copies of the book, including those that Hinman had collated, she found that two of them have the reading "wife," and two others clearly show the crossbar of the *f* in the process of breaking. We find only what we are looking for or are willing to see. Obviously it is a reading whose time has come.

Prospero: Master of Self-knowledge

Barbara Howard Traister

Unlike the magic of plays discussed in earlier chapters [of *Heavenly Nec-romancers*], the nature of the magic in *The Tempest* has received a good deal of critical attention and persuasive explication. Critics have frequently identified Prospero's art as theurgy and often related it to Neoplatonic theories of magic. The intellectual quality of his magic, his command over Ariel (who is clearly daemon, not demon), his concern for astrological guidance, and his use of music in his magic have all been cited to prove his theurgistic and neoplatonic associations. Yet beneath this general chorus of agreement a good deal of disharmony is present. To cite only one example, C. S. Lewis has contended that Prospero's magic is realistic and contemporary, what "might be going on in the next street," while C. J. Sisson asserted in flat contradiction that Prospero's magic is classical and bears little resemblance "to the powers and feats claimed by the professional magicians in contemporary practice." Both observations contain elements of truth: the hybrid nature of Prospero's magic makes it at home in the mysteriously musical and constantly shifting landscape of the island and allows Shakespeare much versatility in its use in the play.

But earlier magical plays have led us to expect hybrid magic; indeed, the most surprising feature of this acknowledged masterpiece among magical plays is how much it shares with and derives from its dramatic forebears. The only unusual features of Prospero as dramatic magician are the success of his magic and his total dominance of the play in which he participates;

From *Heavenly Necromancers: The Magician in English Renaissance Drama.* © 1984 by the Curators of the University of Missouri. University of Missouri Press, 1984.

otherwise he is a rather conventional figure. Far more than Faustus, who captures our attention partly because of his failure to play stereotypical "magician's roles," Prospero displays familiar magical attributes. He is the victor in a magical contest; he commands spirits; he is the director of numerous shows and spectacles; and he assists young love.

I

The magical contest between Prospero and Sycorax is presented with great care, even though it is narrated by Prospero and Ariel and not witnessed by the audience. The "arts" of Sycorax and Prospero competed, not the characters themselves. Indeed, Sycorax was dead before Prospero arrived on the island, so he bears no responsibility for killing or punishing her. His competitive act is thus totally positive: he has freed Ariel from the hollow tree where Sycorax had imprisoned him, a release Sycorax herself had apparently been unable to accomplish. A reminder of the earlier competition (and a grudging admission by an enemy of Prospero's power) is Caliban's testimony that Prospero's "Art is of such pow'r, / It would control my dam's god, Setebos, /And make a vassal of him" (1.2.372–74). In *The Tempest,* as in most plays involving magical competition, the triumph of a given side proves its moral superiority to the magic of the loser, thereby justifying the winner's magic. (Greene's *Friar Bacon* is something of an exception, since Vandermast's magic is not bad or evil, Bacon's victory is nationalistic, not moral.) After all, only Prospero's more powerful "good" magic can counteract the "bad" magic of Sycorax. Shakespeare clearly included this account of Prospero's indirect competition with Sycorax to strengthen Prospero's credentials as a "good" magician.

Another common magical accomplishment is Prospero's ability to command spirits who actually implement his magic. As early as *The Old Wives Tale* and *John a Kent,* spirits aided the magician; Kent's Shrimp is a near relative of Ariel, invisible to all but his magician master and the audience, responsible for shows, for mysterious music, and for leading certain characters astray. Spirits offer evidence of a magician's power and usually suggest the moral value of that power. Shrimp and Ariel, associated with the air and with nature, are morally neutral or even good, while Bacon's spirits and those who pretend to serve Faustus are demonic, servants of the underworld who indicate that the magic they assist is morally dubious or at least dangerous.

Shakespeare carefully depicted the relationship between Ariel and Prospero. Prospero never conjures or ritually summons Ariel onstage; all his bonds of control over the spirit were forged before the play began; onstage a simple command brings Ariel to serve his magician (occasionally with some protest). Ariel's nature and the details by which he is presented make clear that he is drawn in the image of the daemons of Neoplatonic theory, as various critics have pointed out. But his dramatic function is traditional. A beautifully particularized representative of a long line of spirits who serve magicians, Ariel provides spectacle, proof of Prospero's power, and helps explain how the play's magic is performed. Prospero alone is not capable, if he is human, of raising a tempest or of making unearthly music. Only by gaining control of the spirits who manage the functioning of the natural world can a man accomplish what Prospero does; Ariel is a necessary intermediary. As such, he leaves Prospero's humanity intact.

Another traditional role of the magician, one that has tremendous importance in *The Tempest,* is Prospero's function as producer and director of shows. "For what is the magician but, as always in the old plays, a stage manager of shows, with his wand and his magic inscribed 'book'—what is this but a sublimated Master of the Revels?" (M. C. Bradbrook). In fact, virtually the entire *Tempest* is Prospero's production, from the opening storm to the final command to Ariel to provide calm seas and auspicious gales. In no other play is so much of the action preplanned and controlled by a magician. So controlled is Prospero's production that it has led Enid Welsford, for one, to claim that *The Tempest* is more masquelike than *Comus* and to compare Prospero to a masque-presenter.

Within the large structure that Prospero manages, a number of small, self-contained scenes, almost plays-within-the-play, are also directed by Prospero. Such scenes are familiar products of magicians. But, despite the surface conventionality of such "shows" as part of *The Tempest,* their number and their contribution to the thematic movement of the play they adorn are unusual. They differ from John a Kent and John a Cumber's little shows of "antiques" and Friar Bacon's banquet and transportations largely in their thematic integration with the play that contains them. In earlier magical plays, the magician's shows were primarily extraneous entertainments that displayed his magical power. *The Tempest* needs no such demonstration of Prospero's power, but Prospero uses spectacle anyway, for didactic purposes: each little show is especially selected for its audience, and each overturns the initial expectations of that audience in some way. *The Tempest* may be closer to masque than any other Jacobean drama, but its masque elements—used primarily for diversion in many Jacobean plays—are integral to the action and theme of the play as a whole.

Five separate shows appear in *The Tempest.* The first and most spectacular is the opening storm itself, prepared for us all, audience and characters alike. Only Ariel, Prospero, and apparently Caliban are immune to its terror. This is the only show during which Prospero himself does not appear onstage, the only one that the audience does not immediately perceive to be his controlled creation. Like all the other shows, it is designed to surprise, to be other than what it first appears. We discover its illusory nature with Miranda in the second scene; the other characters have yet to hear at the play's end what the tempest was. Prospero's magic in the storm is pure illusion, rearrangement of appearances to play tricks on men's senses, and this is largely the extent of his magic throughout the play. Excepting Ariel's reported release from the tree and Caliban's alleged bruises, Prospero's magic leaves no permanent physical changes. The storm leaves ship, men and garments all "fresher than before" (1.2.219).

Prospero's next three shows are companion pieces, following one another closely in the play and almost inviting comparison. The first such display is the banquet-and-harpy sequence presented to the Neapolitan courtiers as they wander forlornly around the island. Prospero, very much the director of this performance, is "on the top" overseeing both Ariel's performance and his audience's reactions. The beginning of the show is disarmingly pleasant. A banquet is brought on by shapes moving with "gentle actions of salutations" (3.3.18), inviting the men to eat. The banquet gives the illusion of well-being, suggesting what might have been—the joy of friendly communion—had these not been "three men of sin" (3.3.53). But this friendly and gentle beginning is suddenly reversed by the arrival of Ariel as harpy. Immediately the banquet disappears, for these men are not worthy to partake of it. As the tempest was apparently destructive and only later shown to have a good purpose, so the banquet appears welcoming only to be changed abruptly into a scene of warning. Perhaps the whole show figures in little the feast that the three sinners thought they had secured in seizing Prospero's Duchy, a feast that has turned to nothing in their present helpless and powerless position on the island. In any case, Prospero here mixes verbal warning and remonstrance with visible action. The abrupt disappearance of the inviting banquet underlines Ariel's speech, offering evidence that the island brings punishment rather than hospitality to these men.

The care with which Prospero has planned each of his shows is evident when we put beside the banquet-harpy scene the betrothal masque he prepares for Ferdinand and Miranda. Prospero, again onstage directing and supervising the performance of his spirits, calls attention to the close relation between his shows: "I must use you in such another trick," he informs Ariel (4.1.36). The wedding masque differs from its predecessor, however, in emphasizing verbal message over visual spectacle. Ferdinand and Miranda, best of the characters Prospero controls, can respond to poetry and to verbal education as the sin-clogged courtiers cannot. Though visually lovely, the masque conveys its lessons primarily through its verse.

However, its apparent order and beauty are partially qualified, this time, perhaps, against Prospero's own expectation. Just as the horror of the storm and the pleasant invitation of the banquet prove in need of qualification, so the betrothal masque—where "temperate nymphs" and "sunburn'd sickle-men" frolic in perfect harmony together—cannot be allowed a perfect conclusion. Prospero remembers Caliban, who could never have a place in such an ordered vision, and speaks; the spell is "marr'd." Prospero himself cuts short the most perfect and ideal of all the shows he creates, perhaps because he realizes anew that such perfection is only illusion. Clearly, he does not personally fear Caliban's revolt, but recollecting it reminds him that the masque is "baseless fabric" without correspondence to reality. The "show'" prepared for the play's two most promising people must be qualified just like all the other shows—even if against Prospero's will—for Ferdinand and Miranda inhabit a world containing Calibans and Antonios as well as kindly Gonzalos.

However beautiful the wedding masque—however realistic any of Prospero's presentations—it is only a show. Prospero makes no pretense to the lovers that the masque is anything but his own creation, "my present fancies," no pretense that goddesses have actually descended to bless their match. The production is simply Prospero's most impressive way of giving Ferdinand and Miranda his blessing and of conveying to them the proper ideals of love and marriage. It is another of Prospero's didactic messages.

The show for Caliban, Trinculo, and Sebastian immediately follows the masque. It is the simplest and least interesting show in the play, hardly deserving comparison with its predecessors. But it fits the intellectual capabilities of its intended audience. Like the banquet-harpy scene, it has two parts. The first merely displays ornate clothes strung on a line. These gaudy things suit Stephano and Trinculo as the more sophisticated banquet suited the nobles. The clowns seize the clothing and are accosted, in the second part of the show, by Prospero's spirits in the shapes of hunting dogs, set on by Prospero and Ariel. No verbal warning or lesson accompanies this scene, for its audience will not respond to mere words, as Prospero has proved in his experience with Caliban. The thieves, caught red-handed, are punished, immediately and physically. Their lesson must come in the form of pinches and pains—physical discomforts are the only punishment they understand.

Prospero has planned well: he gives each group the show it most deserves and is best able to understand. In each case, the apparent harmony or attractiveness of the opening vision is qualified or negated by what follows. The vision of perfection proffered the lovers is left incomplete. The apparent benevolence of the island toward the nobles is turned to punishment because of their past and present sins. For the clowns, the attractiveness of the glittering clothes they find and seize is quickly shown to be illusory, for their greed leads directly to their deserved punishment. In all these scenes Prospero is present: they are, in effect, his messages to the various groups, made more effective by their dramatic form.

Prospero's final show differs greatly from his earlier ones. Yet its differences help measure the changes that have occurred during the play. Those characters who can repent have done so, and Prospero no longer needs to create didactic illusion. In this final show, Ferdinand and Miranda play chess. Prospero's actors are no longer spirits engaged in pretense but real characters. Prospero presents the lovers with true theatrical flourish. A little like Paulina in *The Winter's Tale,* he builds suspense in his audience. Promising that he will "bring forth a wonder," Prospero steps up to the opening of his cell and, drawing a curtain, reveals the two lovers. His audience expects another magical vision: Alonso, accustomed by now to the illusions and confusions of the place, is not sure whether he sees appearance or reality—"If this prove / A vision of the island, one dear son / Shall I twice lose" (5.1.175–77). Despite Alonso's mistrust, the lovers are real; magic has been abandoned. Its usefulness is over. Magic provided the climate necessary to promote inner changes in Alonso and to control the impulses of the wicked characters. But it is limited in its power to rectify the past and to control the present. It has had and will have no effect on the inner state of those characters who refuse to feel guilt, just as magic has been ineffective in changing human nature in plays previously examined. Ferdinand and Miranda embody Prospero's vision of the future, a future to be shaped by them and by others without the assistance of magic.

Prospero's role as presenter is important, partly because his shows, unlike most magicians' presentations, exist more for their message than for spectacle. Chasing clowns with hunting dogs may appear comparable to Friar Bacon's transportation of Vandermast back to Germany or to Faustus's horning of Benvolio as a rather spectacular and not particularly profound trick. But Prospero is never guilty of purposeless cheap magic, as Bacon and Faustus sometimes are. His understanding of the characters he controls only persuades us more firmly of his wisdom and of the credibility of his magic.

In one other conventional magician's role, Prospero assists, indeed actively promotes, the love affair between his daughter and Ferdinand. Though he has received a good deal of knuckle-rapping from critics for his engineering of the match, Prospero no more controls the inner lives of Ferdinand and Miranda than he controls those of Sebastian and Antonio. He can provide a promising environment, an occasional hurdle or delay, but he has no power to make them love. Prospero is far more personally involved in this match than Peter Fabell, Friar Bungay, or John a Kent are with the affairs in which they interest themselves, but, as in those earlier plays, the magician only facilitates—not creates—the love that brings the play to its happy conclusion.

II

One other aspect of Prospero's magic is often assumed to be traditional, his abjuration of magic and promise to drown his book and break his staff. C. S. Lewis, for example, suggested that a sixteenth-century audience would expect some sort of abjuration: "[Prospero's] speech of renunciation, sometimes taken as an autobiographical confidence by the poet, was to them necessary in order that the ending might be unambiguously happy" (*English Literature in the Sixteenth Century*). Of all the magicians examined, however, only Friar Bacon in *Friar Bacon,* the magicians in *A Looking Glass for London,* Pope Alexander VI in *The Devil's Charter,* and Cyprian in the post-*Tempest* play *The Two Noble Ladies* repent or abjure their magic. Of these, all but Friar Bacon have used magic for clearly evil purposes. Contrarily, benevolent magicians who do not repent or renounce magic include Bomelio in *The Rare Triumphs of Love & Fortune,* John a Kent, Friar Bacon in *John of Bordeaux,* and Peter Fabell in *The Merry Devil of Edmonton.* Abjuration was clearly not essential for magicians, although enough precedents in magical literature exist to make abjuration something an audience might rather expect than not. Yet Prospero's abjuration does not appear to be merely a pro forma bow to audience expectation, even though, of all the magicians I have surveyed, he seems to have the least reason to renounce magic. He has made no errors with his "art" (as Bacon had), nor has he overtly challenged the power of God (as had other repentant magicians). His obvious mistake in emphasizing his studies to the neglect of his civic responsibilities lies outside the play, but only through his magic is he now able to begin to rectify that earlier error.

To understand Prospero's decision to abandon the magic that apparently serves him well, we must recognize his abjuration as a vital part of his overall plan. It is not an impulse of the moment. From the first act he has promised Ariel his freedom within two days, and for Prospero to continue to practice magic without Ariel is unimaginable. A number of critics, however, searching for dramatic tension in the play, locate the conflict within Prospero himself and believe that the drama's principal action is his change from an initial desire for revenge to his later forgiveness of his enemies. For that forgiveness, Ariel's speech at the beginning of act 5 is frequently taken as the catalyst. D. G. James, for example, wrote, "In place of magic forgiveness comes now. Prospero's forgiveness does not come easily or readily. He needed to be instigated to it, we remark, by Ariel; and when he expresses it, he does so not without a touch of prig-gishness." Since, moreover, Prospero's soliloquy abjuring magic follows immediately after Ariel's speech, critics frequently assume a cause-and-effect relationship between the two speeches. Thus Norman Rabkin commented that Prospero's "movement to the benign and charitable renunciation of the last act is a spiritual revolution that we watch on stage." But surely Prospero's benevolence toward his enemies has been obvious from the first act. Not only his promise to free Ariel but also his concern not to harm the courtiers in any way and to keep their ship in good condition suggest that Prospero's intentions go far beyond sterile revenge and that he has planned from the beginning to give up his magic, forgive his enemies, and return with them to Milan. For what other reason would he have hoped for the marriage of Ferdinand and Miranda even before their first meeting? The only uncertainty about Prospero's intentions is how long he will let the courtiers suffer before releasing them from their madness, and Ariel's report of their condition and near pity for them prompts Prospero to release them at once.

Prospero's renunciation of magic is a well-considered choice, consonant with his other actions in the play, for Prospero knows the limits of his power. His decision to abandon magic is part of a primary theme of *The Tempest*: the limits to which man is subject and how he may best work within them. Limits upon men, or, more precisely, on magicians, have been a theme of nearly all the magical plays here considered: Sacrapant could not control himself, though he could control others; Greene's Bacon overstepped the bounds of proper magic by the egocentricity of his magical ambitions; Pope Alexander's magic allowed him to view events but not to control them; Faustus's grand desires were much curbed by the limits Me-phistopeles imposed. At first glance, Prospero seems unfettered by the restrictions that other magicians encountered, for everything (except, per-haps, the wedding masque) goes as he has planned. Yet he is successful primarily because he knows his limitations and works productively within them. Prospero cooperates with nature, as Northrop Frye has pointed out:

"Prospero's magic is an identification with nature as a power rather than as an order or harmony, and is expressed in images of time rather than space, music rather than architecture. Like all magicians, he observes time closely . . . and his charms are effective only if he follows the rhythm of time." Close observation of time is certainly characteristic of Prospero, though perhaps not of "all" magicians. His reiterated concern with time (see, for example, in 1.2 alone, lines 23, 37, 50, 237–40, and so on), his expressed need to accomplish his entire scheme within four hours, is not simply a gratuitous whim. The moment most propitious to his action is at hand, and he must use it well:

> By accident most strange, bountiful Fortune
> (Now my dear lady) hath mine enemies
> Brought to this shore; and by my prescience
> I find my zenith doth depend upon
> A most auspicious star, whose influence
> If now I court not, but omit, my fortunes
> Will ever after droop.
>
> (1.2.178–84)

Working with auspicious astrological signs, anxious to complete his work before those signs change, Prospero has to be time-conscious; his power depends on utilizing time properly.

Though Prospero has prepared carefully for the moment, he finds magical control hard to sustain, and the possibility of failure is always present. Robert West claimed that Prospero is "tense with doubts that he alone among the characters can feel and that a modern audience probably appreciates much less than a Jacobean one did." Though his doubts do not seem to weigh upon him all that heavily, Prospero's concern that his spells are working well explains why he questions Ariel so carefully about the success of the tempest, why he is so delighted to see Ferdinand and Miranda falling in love, and why he reiterates that everything is going according to plan:

> My high charms work,
> And these, mine enemies, are all knit up
> In their distractions.
>
> (3.3.88–90)

> Now does my project gather to a head:
> My charms crack not; my spirits obey; and Time
> Goes upright with his carriage.
>
> (5.1.1–3)

Perhaps the best way to emphasize how wrong things could have gone is to remember Faustus, who paid no attention to the proper time but hurried his attempts at magic, whose spirits did not obey, or rather obeyed only under certain conditions, and whose initial projects were never carried out. Unlike Faustus, Prospero knows how to admit and accept limitations, even such a limitation as Caliban exemplifies. For Prospero is limited by more than time and the possibility of his magic going awry. Even at its most potent, magic has no power to alter men's souls, to civilize a Caliban or to bring an Antonio to repentance. This limitation, too, is familiar from other magical plays; usually it occurs in cases where love potions are ineffective because no magic can force a woman's love (as in *John of Bordeaux, The Wars of Cyrus,* and *The Two Noble Ladies*). This limitation, especially with regard to Caliban, Prospero accepts with much less grace than other restrictions. He is angry that Caliban cannot be reformed, cannot be molded according to Prospero's own notion of goodness. But by the play's end he is willing to acknowledge Caliban and to take responsibility for him as he is: "This thing of darkness I / Acknowledge mine" (5.1.275–76). The hardest of all limitations to bear, the impossibility of improving those unwilling to be improved, is finally accepted by Prospero.

But he has not always understood about limitations. He committed errors in the past, as he admits to Miranda when he narrates to her their history:

> I, thus neglecting worldly ends, all dedicated
> To closeness and the bettering of my mind
> With that which, but by being so retir'd,
> O'er-priz'd all popular rate, in my false brother
> Awak'd an evil nature, and my trust,
> Like a good parent, did beget of him
> A falsehood in its contrary, as great
> As my trust was, which had indeed no limit,
> A confidence sans bound.
>
> (1.2.89–97)

Prospero reveals himself twice guilty in recounting his tale. First, he "neglect[ed] . . . worldly ends." By throwing himself into his studies, being "rapt" and "transported," Prospero was guilty of upsetting the proper balance between contemplation and action. His second mistake was also one of excess, of trusting without limits, which in turn produced Antonio's betrayal "sans bound." Clearly, Prospero was partly to blame for his own deposition, and he has learned much about control and balance in twelve years on the island. Much of the play's interest lies in the way Prospero uses power: once before he used it badly; now the questions are whether he can keep it within bounds and whether he will use it wisely for general good instead of for selfish ends. Power corrupts; it corrupted Antonio and Alonso twelve years before their island sojourn; it corrupts Sebastian and Trinculo and Stephano before our eyes. Magicians in other plays have been ruined by a desire for power: Bacon's magic becomes dangerous when he tries to use it to enhance his own reputation, and Faustus is corrupted by his longing to be a demigod. We are fascinated to watch Prospero, who has more power than any of the others, to see if he can hold to his benevolent purpose. We note his occasional irritation, the desire he naturally has, and once or twice expresses, for revenge, and wait to see if he will falter. But he never does. Obviously, Prospero has changed from the naively trusting and "rapt" scholar of Milan. But his change took place before the shipwreck, and the play unfolds as a perfect example of that control and balance, that proper use of magic and its results, however precariously maintained, which Prospero has learned in his exile.

The play's concern with the limits and boundaries to which man is subject explains, without resorting to allegory, several of the problems critics have raised about the play. The emphasis on chastity that Prospero reiterates to the lovers, for example, has earned him such labels as *busybody* and *prig,* but he is simply admonishing Ferdinand about the importance of self-control—"do not give dalliance / Too much the rein" (4.1.51–52)—and of observing the rules of the marriage ritual in which he is soon to participate. Nothing shows more clearly Prospero's rage for order than the betrothal masque he creates: measured, harmonious, and to be completed by a dance. Prospero's didactic attitude toward the young lovers may offend some critics, but he is merely trying to teach the lessons of controls and limits less harshly than he himself has been forced to learn them. One indication that he has been effective (or perhaps that his lesson was unnecessary) is the lovers' choice, in the final scene, of a game of chess, highly structured with many rules and, according to Kermode, an accepted pastime for noble lovers. Even here, Miranda's protestations that no matter what Ferdinand does she will call it "fair play" suggest that she still has much to learn about the world.

The references to innocence and naiveté that permeate the play take on some negative connotations once we learn in scene 2 that it was his confidence "sans bound" that lost Prospero his Duchy. Miranda is the most positive of the naive characters, fully willing to see everyone and everything from the civilized world as wonderful. Only about Caliban, the one being besides her father whom she knows well, does Miranda have negative opinions: "Abhorred slave! / Which any print of goodness will not take" (1.2.351–52). This appraisal of Caliban suggests that Miranda is educable about the evil to be found in the world, and despite her naive outburst at the sight of the less than noble courtiers—"O brave new world / That has such people in it" (5.1.183–84)—we respond positively to her enthusiasm, knowing that she has as protectors people more knowledgeable about the world than she.

The other chief "innocent" of the play is Gonzalo, the unfailing optimist, forever ready to find good in all people and events. But though he is clearly one of the play's good characters, his judgment is not to be trusted. Unlike Miranda, Gonzalo has had plenty of opportunity to witness the world's evil—it was he, after all, who supervised the banishment of Prospero—and still he has not learned. Gonzalo's optimism is balanced perfectly by the cynicism and pessimism of Sebastian and Antonio. Though Gonzalo is a far better person than they, his unqualified exuberance is as much an excess as their materialistic cynicism. Nowhere is this excess more evident than in Gonzalo's utopian fantasy of a world where, as he stresses, there are to be no boundaries, no limits:

> for no kind of traffic
> Would I admit; no name of magistrate;
> Letters should not be known; riches, poverty,
> And use of service, none; contract, succession,
> Bourn, bound of land, tilth, vineyard, none.
>   (2.1.149–53)

The response of the play's various characters to the apparent lack of control on the island—Sebastian and Antonio's plot of fratricide and regicide; Stephano and Trinculo's mounting ambition to rule; Caliban's murderous plans—immediately negates Gonzalo's vision. Such innocence as his is dangerous, no matter how appealing. Trusting to Providence completely and doing nothing for oneself is a kind of sloth of which one increasingly suspects Gonzalo to be guilty. Prospero, once trusting like Gonzalo, but now active and no longer "rapt," understands the need to be alert to evil.

The delicate set of balances on which *The Tempest* is poised has been noted repeatedly. But the balance most crucial to an understanding of Prospero's renunciation of magic is the balance in the play between the human and the nonhuman.

Just as *The Tempest* examines the limits of innocence, so does it treat the limits of humanity. Several times in the play Shakespeare calls attention to the problem of defining the human. Miranda mistakes Ferdinand for a spirit; he mistakes her for a goddess (1.2). Caliban thinks Stephano and Trinculo are Prospero's spirits come to punish him, while they mistake him for a fish and a monster (2.2). Gonzalo assumes the spirits who serve the banquet are "people of the island" (3.3). All of these mistakes draw attention to the need to identify what is human.

Moreover, several characters embody in themselves a duality. Caliban—"man-monster," "servant-monster," "misshapen knave," and "demi-devil"—has no certain place on the scale of being; no one can decide whether he is man or beast. His animal instincts are always foremost, but he is human enough to have learned language and, by the play's end, to despise his drunken companions and resolve to sue for grace. In some ways Ariel, too, is almost human. Unlike the largely silent spirits over whom he has charge, Ariel delights in language. He has long talks with Prospero, arguing with him or complimenting him very much as a human being might. This element of Ariel's character is made clearest, of course, at the beginning of act 5, when he describes the pitiful condition of the courtiers and avers that he would pity them "were I human" (5.1.19).

But Prospero himself provides the most crucial test in the play of what it is to be human. Throughout, he acts much like a god while at the same time maintaining his human roles as father to Miranda and as the wronged ruler of Milan. Onstage, the duality of Prospero's nature is signaled clearly by the donning and doffing of his magician's cloak. Whenever Prospero is acting as a magician—immediately after the tempest, in his conversations with Ariel, when he produces his magical shows—he is dressed in the cloak. When he is involved in human relationships—the talk with Miranda, probably when he gives the lovers his blessing before their masque, and at the play's end when he forgives his enemies—Prospero is without the cloak. In the last scene, he wears his ducal clothing, symbolic of the role of governor that he lost and now is to reassume. It is this final change of clothes that signals once and for all that Prospero has tipped the delicate balance he has maintained throughout the play; he has chosen to be human and not godlike.

In Neoplatonic theory, of course, the aim of the magician was to gain knowledge, to strip himself of the concerns of the world, and, in effect, to abandon his flawed and earthbound humanity. Walter Clyde Curry described this process:

> Mere man may control irrational daemons in the practice of goetical art; but when his soul has been elevated to the point

> where he commands aerial daemons, then he is able to control
> mundane natures, not as man but as theurgist. He now makes
> use of greater mandates than pertain to himself as man. As his
> soul passes further through the spheres of ethereal and celestial
> daemons, his mystic powers become greater and more god-like.
> And finally, when he is completely assimilated to the gods, he
> becomes impassive like them and is able to exercise all the powers
> of the gods themselves. . . . Theurgical practices . . . represent
> no more than a means of preparation for the intellectual soul in
> its upward progress; union with the intelligible gods is the
> theurgist's ultimate aim.

In this scheme of things, there is no place for a return to worldly affairs or
to humanity. Impassivity suggests remoteness; Curry felt that this is the
state that Prospero achieved. Other critics also have seen Prospero achieving
perfect harmony by the play's end so that "rough magic" is no longer
necessary for him. Hardin Craig, for example, commented, "Prospero can
burn his book and drown his staff, for they are no longer needed, for he
has become perfect in himself as a single, separate, completely powerful
and educated man." But things are hardly so perfect at the play's end:
Sebastian and Antonio show no evidence of reform, and Prospero silences
them only by threatening to reveal their plot to Alonso; Caliban, though
he says he will sue for grace, is still Caliban; and Prospero is going back
to wrestle with a job in which he once failed miserably.

Prospero's choice—to return to Milan, to resume his worldly position,
and to abjure magic—is a choice to remain human, despite all the weakness
and danger human beings are subject to. He will use the wisdom gained
from his books and from his experience on the island in the world of flux
where he has human ties. To have retained his magic and continued on the
path to wisdom mapped out by the Neoplatonists would have been to
become the impassive, godlike figure of Curry's description. But Prospero
is acutely aware of his human responsibilities and of his human limits, his
susceptibility to time, and chooses to remain where "Every third thought
shall be my grave."

In some ways his decision resembles Bussy D'Ambois's refusal to reach
beyond the world for knowledge. He resembles, too, one neoplatonist
magician who did not subscribe to the impassivity and aloofness expected
of the philosopher-magician. In his "Preface" to Henry Billingsley's translation of Euclid's *Elements*, John Dee described the natural philosopher (and
hence the theurgistic magician, though Dee would not have dared to use
those words):

Thus, can the Mathematicall minde, deal Speculatiuely in his own Arte: and by good meanes, Mount aboue the cloudes and sterres; and thirdly, he can, by order, Descend, to frame Naturall thinges, to wonderfull vses: and when he list, retire home into his owne Centre: and there, prepare more Meanes, to Ascend or Descend by: and, all, to the glory of God and our honest delectation in earth.

Much as Dee described the duty of "the Mathematicall minde," so Prospero has learned to control the extraterrestrial world for the benefit of humanity. As Dee urged, he not only ascends to wisdom but also descends again to apply it. Thus he is unlike the Neoplatonic theorizers for whom magic was a means of escape to other worlds of knowledge and resembles rather the earnest English scientist and magician who tried to put theory into practice to "the end of well doing, and not of well knowing only." For his efforts at practical magic, Dee earned a reputation as a quack. But perhaps, to Shakespeare and his contemporaries, Dee appeared more like Prospero, a man of wisdom and power who devoted his talents to bettering his world.

Thus, Prospero knows from the play's beginning the boundaries of his art and knows, too, that at a certain point he must renounce it. Having learned both magical and self-control, he halts his progress upward, refusing to climb further, to become more than man, for he is "one of their kind" (5.1.23).

III

Prospero's decision to limit his magic, confining it to a certain sphere of action, is echoed by the structure of *The Tempest* itself. The play has long been recognized as metadramatic, chiefly because of Prospero's "revels" speech and the epilogue, both of which force metadramatic recognitions. And, of course, the identification of Prospero with Shakespeare, of one's magic with the other's drama, is still tempting to many. Apart from reference to Shakespeare's biography, however, the play calls attention to itself as play in a number of ways.

Among its most important metadramatic elements is the similarity between the limits that Prospero imposes on his magic and those the playwright places on his play. Though most critics comment on the play's observance of the three unities, no one has offered a convincing dramatic explanation for their presence. L. G. Salingar has spoken of "the sense of difficulty overcome," and Bernard Knox has remarked that "the fantasy and originality of the setting must be balanced and disciplined by a rigid adherence to tradition." But such comments are inadequate. In this play about a creative magician who works within the limits of his magic and his humanity, Shakespeare has undertaken to demonstrate that he, too, can work within limits traditionally prescribed for drama by classical theory. Magic and dramatic creation are similar; form matches content; magician and dramatist both work gracefully within the boundaries of their art.

A concern with limits is not the only similarity between the playwright and Prospero, between drama and magic. Prospero functions for Shakespeare to give the play its comic structure. He plans his action carefully so that gradually the three groups of characters he controls approach a common spot, the area in front of his cell. Ferdinand is admitted there almost at once, as the suitor of Miranda, but the courtiers come only after much trial and wandering. The clowns—who first come too soon and with intent to murder Prospero—are driven away, only to be summoned again for judgment in the last moments of the play. Like any good comic dramatist, Prospero gathers his entire cast onstage for the finale so that proper rewards and punishments may be meted out. Shakespeare used Prospero to accomplish his own purposes, for he too needed all present in order to end *The Tempest.* Prospero thus makes plausible within the fiction of the play the mechanical manipulation necessary to end it. The dramatist and his chief character function together as smoothly as Prospero and Ariel.

Finally, of course, the language and imagery of the play continually insist upon its metadramatic implications. Like drama, magic is always a temporary illusion in *The Tempest*—an "insubstantial pageant." This is true of magic in most of the plays previously examined; the illusion that magic provides and the magician's frequent provision of shows have almost always had metadramatic undertones. In *The Tempest,* however, the associations with drama, always latent in the conventions of Renaissance stage magic, are fully developed. The art of magic and the art of dramaturgy are inextricably entwined, their similarities highly developed. Prospero's magic is primarily illusion; so is theater. Yet each has possibilities for educating, for momentarily so altering perceptible reality that audiences may, like Alonso, be impelled toward self-examination. In *The Tempest,* magic has the power to frighten, to instruct, to delight—all powers possessed by drama, as well. Though its metadramatic association is not the only function of magic in Shakespeare's play, or necessarily its primary one, magic's dramatic potential—present but incompletely realized in many earlier magical plays— is here given full development and adds a good deal to the richness of Shakespeare's play.

The Tempest is the culminating treatment not only of magic's metadramatic possibilities but of other of its thematic associations as well. The play presents the most complete picture of the positive potential of magic we have seen. While *Faustus* shows magic at its lowest, as a trick the devil uses to ensnare a human soul by deceptive promises of power, *The Tempest* reveals magic at its most powerful, used carefully by a man who understands its limits and does not twist it for his own egotistical satisfactions. Greene's *Friar Bacon* implies that such magic is possible, but in Greene's play magic is skewed by Bacon's pride and his misunderstanding of the proper use of his power.

Concomitant with its careful presentation of magic (purposefully kept vague as to details so that there might be nothing concrete to criticize) is *The Tempest*'s examination of the man who practices it. Prospero makes no mistakes as a magician, has no flaws in his magic that might explain why magic does not make him forever omnipotent. Thus Prospero becomes the supreme embodiment on the English stage of the paradoxical figure of the magician: a man of great power who can force or influence nature to alter her course for him, but a man nonetheless limited who is, finally, not a god, only human, and thus faces boundaries beyond which he must not pass. Such limitations characterize almost all dramatic magicians from Sacrapant and Bomelio to Bacon and Faustus (a few minor exceptions, such as Bacon in *John of Bordeaux* and Merlin in *The Birth of Merlin,* apparently have no restrictions whatsoever). Yet always some extraneous reason prevents the magician from reaching the full development one might expect from his powers: he is a minor character and not fully realized in the play; he stands in opposition to God and thus cannot achieve anything significant; he has a flaw—pride, lust, haste—that makes him pervert his magic to unworthy ends. None of these excuses for limitation characterizes Prospero. Yet he embodies the paradox of superhuman power that is humanly limited.

This very paradox, I suspect, made the magician an attractive figure for some English dramatists. The emphasis on the humanity of the magicians created for the stage is, after all, the feature that most distinguishes them from the freakish caricatures who are the magicians in medieval narrative romances. Knowing that some of their contemporaries regarded magic as dangerous, unholy, or the work of the devil and that others— including some of Europe's leading intellectuals—saw it as a positive means of attaining wisdom and power with which to better the world, dramatists may have fastened upon magic, perhaps unconsciously, as an ideal image for conveying one view of man's place in the universe. The dominant thrust of Renaissance thought emphasized that man had great power to shape and change himself and his world; he was "the great Amphibian" or the "chameleon" who could rise almost to the height of the angels or fall almost to the level of the beasts. What better way to express man's potential than through the image of magic, as Pico did in his *Oration?* And what better way to express the frustrating fact that, however, great his powers, man could never escape the weakness and fallibility of his humanity than by emphasizing the limitations on those magical powers, which promise much but can be carried only to the limits of mortality?

"This Thing of Darkness I Acknowledge Mine": *The Tempest* and the Discourse of Colonialism

Paul Brown

It has long been recognised that *The Tempest* bears traces of the contemporary British investment in colonial expansion. Attention has been drawn to Shakespeare's patronal relations with prominent members of the Virginia Company and to the circumstances of the play's initial production at the expansionist Jacobean court in 1611 and 1612–13. Borrowings from a traditional and classical stock of exotic stereotypes, ranging from the wild man, the savage and the masterless man to the tropology of the pastoral *locus amoenus* and the wilderness, have been noted. Semi-quotations from contemporary propagandist pamphlets and Montaigne's essay on cannibals have been painstakingly logged. However, a sustained historical and theoretical analysis of the play's involvement in the colonialist project has yet to be undertaken. This chapter seeks to demonstrate that *The Tempest* is not simply a reflection of colonialist practices but an intervention in an ambivalent and even contradictory discourse. This intervention takes the form of a powerful and pleasurable narrative which seeks at once to harmonise disjunction, to transcend irreconcilable contradictions and to mystify the political conditions which demand colonialist discourse. Yet the narrative ultimately fails to deliver that containment and instead may be seen to foreground precisely those problems which it works to efface or overcome. The result is a radically ambivalent text which exemplifies not some *timeless* contradiction internal to the discourse by which it inexorably

From *Political Shakespeare: New Essays in Cultural Materialism,* edited by Jonathan Dollimore and Alan Sinfield. © 1985 by Paul Brown. Manchester University Press, 1985.

undermines or deconstructs its "official" pronouncements, but a moment of *historical* crisis. This crisis is the struggle to produce a coherent discourse adequate to the complex requirements of British colonialism in its initial phase. Since accounts of the miraculous survival of members of the company of the Sea Adventure, wrecked off Bermuda in 1609, are said to have provided Shakespeare with an immediate source for his production, let an incident in the later life of one of those survivors serve as a ground for this analysis.

In 1614 John Rolfe, a Virginia planter, wrote a letter seeking the Governor's blessing for his proposed marriage with Pocahontas, abducted daughter of Powhatan, chief-of-chiefs. This remarkable document announces a victory for the colonialist project, confirming Rolfe in the position of coloniser and Pocahontas in the position of a savage other. The letter is an exposure of Rolfe's inner motives to public scrutiny, a production of his civilised "self" as a text to be read by his superiors, that is, his Governor and his God. What lurks in Rolfe's "secret bosome" is a desire for a savage female. He has had "to strive with all my power of body and minde, in the undertaking of so mightie a matter, no way led (so farre forth as mans weaknesse may permit) with the unbridled desire of carnall affection: but for the good of this plantation, for the honour of our countrie, for the glory of God, for my own salvation, and for the converting to the true knowledge of God and Jesus Christ, an unbeleeving creature, namely Pokahuntas." As the syntax of the sentence indicates, the whole struggle, fought on the grounds of psychic order, social cohesion, national destiny, theological mission, redemption of the sinner and the conversion of the pagan, is conducted in relation to the female body. "Carnall affection" would appear, despite Rolfe's disavowal, to have been a force which might disrupt commitments to conscience, Governor and God.

Pocahontas had posed a problem that was "so intricate a laborinth, that I was even awearied to unwinde my selfe thereout." Yet whether good or evil, Pocahontas cannot fail to operate as a sign of Rolfe's election, since if reformable, she is the space to be filled with the saintly seed of civility, if obdurately irreformable, she assures the godliness of him who is called to trial (the whole ethos of the godly community in the wilderness depended upon such proximity and exposure to evil). Rolfe's supposedly problematic letter may therefore be said to *produce* Pocahontas as an other in such a way that she will always affirm Rolfe's sense of godly duty and thus confirm him as a truly civil subject.

Inexorably, the text moves from the possible beleaguerments of carnality—variously constituted as the threat of the tempting wilderness, the charge that Rolfe's own interests in this matter are purely sexual, and the possible detraction of "depravers and turbulent spirits" within the colony—towards a more positive presentation. Now the carnal affection which might fracture Rolfe's sense of duty becomes reencoded as a vital part of God's commandments: "why was I created? If not for transitory pleasures and worldly vanities, but to labour in the Lord's vineyard, there to sow and plant, to nourish and increase the fruites thereof, daily adding with the good husbandman in the Gospell, somewhat to the tallent, that in the end the fruites may be reaped, to the comfort of the laborer in this life, and his salvation in the world to come?" Given this imperative, mutual sexual desire, including the female's "own inticements," can be admitted. Now it would be unmasterly not to desire her, as husbandman. The other incites the godly project: the godly project is embodied in the other. With the word thus made flesh and with Rolfe's self-acquittal in the court of conscience, all that remains to be achieved is the reorientation of those potential detractors into public witnesses of Rolfe's heroism, that "all the world may truly say: this is the work of God, and it is marvelous in our eies."

The threats of disruption to Rolfe's servitude to conscience, Governor and God have thus become the site of the affirmation of psychic, social and cosmic order. The encounter with the savage other serves to confirm the civil subject in that self-knowledge which ensures self-mastery. Of his thoughts and desires he can say: "I know them all, and have not rashly overslipped any." The letter, then, rehearses the power of the civil subject to maintain self-control and to bring the other into his service, even as it refers to a desire which might undermine that mastery.

After his initial calls for Rolfe to be denounced as a traitor, James I allowed the "princess," newly christened "Lady Rebecca," into court as visible evidence of the power of civility to transform the other. Pocahontas was to die in England a nine days' wonder; Rolfe returned to his tobacco plantation, to be killed in the great uprising of the Indians in 1622. The Pocahontas myth was only beginning, however.

Even this partial analysis of one aspect of such myth-making serves to demonstrate the characteristic operations of the discourse of colonialism. This complex discourse can be seen to have operated in two main areas: they may be called "masterlessness" and "savagism." Masterlessness analyses wandering or unfixed and unsupervised elements located in the internal margins of civil society (in the above example, Rolfe's subjective desire and potential detractors within the colony). Savagism probes and categorises alien cultures on the external margins of expanding civil power (in the same example, the Amerindian cultures of Virginia). At the same time as they serve to define the other, such discursive practices refer back to those conditions which constitute civility itself. Masterlessness reveals the mastered (submissive, observed, supervised, deferential) and masterful (powerful, observing, supervising, teleological) nature of civil society. Savagism (asociality and untrammelled libidinality) reveals the necessity of psychic and institutional order and direction in the civil regime. In practice these two concepts are intertwined and mutually reinforcing. Together they constitute a powerful discourse in which the noncivil is represented to the civil subject to produce for Rolfe a "laborinth" out of which, like Theseus escaping from the Minotaur's lair, he is to "unwinde" his "selfe."

That such an encounter of the civil and noncivil should be couched in terms of the promulgation/resistance of fulfilling/destructive sexual desire, as it is in Rolfe's case, deserves careful attention, as this strategy is common in colonialist discourse. Such tropes as that of the coloniser as husbandman making the land fruitful, or of the wilderness offering a dangerous libidinal attraction to the struggling saint, are ubiquitous. The discourse of sexuality in fact offers the crucial nexus for the various domains of colonialist discourse which I have schematised above. Rolfe's letter reorients potentially truant sexual desire within the confines of a duly ordered and supervised civil relationship. *The Tempest* represents a politicisation of what for Rolfe is experienced as primarily a crisis of his individual subjectivity. For example, the proof of Prospero's power to order and supervise his little colony is manifested in his capacity to control not *his,* but his *subjects'* sexuality, particularly that of his slave and his daughter. Rolfe's personal triumph of reason over passion or soul over body is repeated publicly as Prospero's triumphant ordering of potentially truant or subversive desires in his body politic. Similarly, Prospero's reintegration into the political world of Milan and Naples is represented, in Prospero's narrative, as an elaborate courtship, a series of strategic manoeuvres with political as well as "loving" intentions and effects. This will be examined further in due course. For the moment I am simply seeking to show connection between a class discourse (masterlessness), a race discourse (savagism) and a courtly and politicised discourse on sexuality. This characteristically produces an encounter with the other involving the coloniser's attempts to dominate, restrict, and exploit the other even as that other offers allurements which might erode the order obtaining within the civil subject or the body politic. This encounter is truly a labyrinthine situation, offering the affirmation or *ravelling up* of the civil subject even as it raises the possibility of its undoing, its erosion, its *unravelling.* A brief survey of British colonial operations will help us to establish a network of relations or discursive matrix *within and against which* an analysis of *The Tempest* becomes possible.

Geographically, the discourse operated upon the various domains of British world influence, which may be discerned roughly, in the terms of Immanuel Wallerstein, as the "core," "semiperiphery" and "periphery." Colonialism therefore comprises the expansion of royal hegemony in the English-Welsh mainland (the internal colonialism of the core), the extension of British influence in the semiperiphery of Ireland, and the diffuse range of British interests in the extreme periphery of the New World. Each expansive thrust extended British power beyond existing spheres of influence into new margins. In the core, these areas included the North, Wales and other "dark corners" such as woods, wastes and suburbs. In the semiperiphery, the Pale around Dublin was extended and other areas subdued and settled. In America, official and unofficial excursions were made into "virgin" territory. I have given one example of the production of an American other; the production of core and Irish others will exemplify the enormous scope of contemporary colonialist discourse.

In his "archaeology" of the wild man type, Hayden White discusses the threat to civil society posed by the very proximity of antisocial man: "he is just out of sight, over the horizon, in the nearby forest, desert, mountains, or hills. He sleeps in crevices, under great trees, or in the caves of wild animals" (in *The Wild Man Within,* edited by Edward Dudley and Maximillian Novak). Many of these characteristics are shared by the more socially specific production of the "masterless man," the ungoverned and unsupervised man without the restraining resources of social organisation, an embodiment of directionless and indiscriminate desire. Masterless types were discerned in royal proclamations to exist in the very suburbs of the capital. These and other texts produce a counterculture within the margins of civility, living in disorder, requiring surveillance, classification, expulsion and punishment. A typical example is Richard Johnson's *Look Upon Me London* (1613) in which warnings against the city's many "alectives to unthriftinesse" are given. To counter such traps for the ingenuous sons of the gentry, Johnson produces a taxonomy of bad houses, hierarchically arranged according to the social standing of their clientele, of which the worst are "out of the common walkes of the magistrates." These are "privy houses," privy in that they are hidden and secret and also in that they attract the dirt or excremental elements of the body politic. Such dirt is continually viewed as a dire threat to civil order in this literature. Johnson specifically warns that "if the shifters in, and within the level of London, were truly mustered, I dare boldly say they would amaze a good army." The masterless are, here, produced as an other, that "many-headed multitude" common in such writing.

This other is a threat around which the governing classes might mob-

ilise, that is, around which they might recognise their common class position, as governors, over and against the otherwise ungoverned and
dangerous multitudes. In *The Tempest* Stephano the "drunken butler" and
the "jester" Trinculo obviously represent such masterless men, whose al-
liance with the savage Caliban provides an antitype of order, issuing in a
revolt requiring chastisement and ridicule. The assembled aristocrats in the
play, and perhaps in the original courtly audiences, come to recognise in
these figures their own common identity—and the necessity for a solidarity
among the ruling class in face of such a threat. This solidarity must take
priority over any internecine struggles; the masterless therefore function to
bind the rulers together in hegemony. They were produced as a counter-
order, sometimes classified according to rigid hierarchies of villainy in some
demonic parody of good order, sometimes viewed as a reserve army of
potential recruits for rebellion sometimes offered as a mere negative principle, the simple absence of the requirements of civility, attracting the sons
of the gentry through its very spaciousness, irresponsibility and dirtiness.

Johnson's text produces a complex pleasure beyond the simple production of an instrumental knowledge of the masterless other. This knowledge is certainly offered for the services of magistracy and no doubt produces
the antitype by which good order might be defined. Yet this moral and
serviceable discourse displays in its descriptive richness precisely the intense
and voyeuristic fascination for the other which it warns the gentry against.
The text ostensibly avoids the taint of voyeurism by declaring that since
this probing and exposing of dirt is required for the sober gaze of magistracy, a certain specular pleasure may be allowed. Again, at least officially,
a potentially disruptive desire provoked by the "alective" other of masterlessness is channelled into positive civil service. This encoding of pleasure
within the production of useful knowledge for the advantage of civil power
is specifically described by Francis Bacon in his essay "Of Truth" as an
erotic and courtly activity: the pursuit of knowledge is a "love-making or
wooing." Bacon implicitly offers an ideal of Renaissance sovereignty which
can unite what Foucault terms "power-knowledge-pleasure." Here pleasure
is not simply disruptive, something produced by the other to deform or
disturb the civil subject; it is a vital adjunct to power, a utilisation of the
potentially disruptive to further the workings of power. In courtly fictions
we can see this movement in operation: the other is incorporated into the
service of sovereignty by reorienting *its* desires.

Such fictions include celebrations which centre upon the figure of the
good sovereign. In these, the mere presence of the royal personage and the
power of the royal gaze are able to transmute hitherto recalcitrant elements

of the body politic, engendering in the place of disorderly passion a desire for service that is akin to an erotic courtship. In progresses, processions and masques such powers were continually complimented. In 1575, for example, at Kenilworth, Elizabeth I was confronted by an "Hombre Salvagio." In dangerous marginal space, beyond the confines of the great house, at the edge of the wild woods, at a most dangerous hour (nine o'clock in the evening), the Virgin Queen encountered the very emblem of marginality. But at this moment of maximum threat the wild man is metamorphosed into her eloquent and loving subject. He says:

> O queen, I must confesse it is not without cause
> These civile people so rejoice, that you should give them
> lawes.
> Since I, which live at large, a wilde and savage man,
> And have ronne out a wilfull race, since first my life began,
> Do here submit my selfe, beseeching yow to serve.

The Hombre's entry into a loving relationship with Elizabeth is also his entry into interpersonal language (he has hitherto only spoken to his echo) and into subjection to a lawful sovereign: his very capacity to represent himself as "I" is in the gift of the sovereign. She confers on him the status of a linguistic and a legal subject, he now operates in a courtly idiom and in the "sentence" of the sovereign law. Such taming of the wild man by a courtly virgin is a ubiquitous trope in medieval and Renaissance literature, as Richard Bernheimer has shown. It serves as an emblem of courtly power, of the capacity to reorient masterlessness and savagism into service without recourse to the naked exercise of coercive power. This tropology is of great importance in the delineation of the Miranda—Caliban relationship, as I shall show later.

The discourse of masterlessness was embodied also in proclamations and statutes requiring that the bodies of vagrant classes, for example, should be modified. Those condemned as persistent vagrants could literally be marked (whipped, bored, branded) with public signs announcing their adulteration, the hallmark of vice. Alternatively they could suffer the discipline of the work-house or the Bridewell. Yet no apparatus seemed sufficient to keep their numbers down. The constant vilification and punishment of those designated masterless by the ruling classes was not simply a strategy designed to legitimate civil rule: it also evidences a genuine anxiety. This took several forms: a real fear of the power of the governed classes should they mobilise against their betters; a complex displacement of the fear of aristocratic revolt on to the already vilified; a realisation that the increasing numbers of mobile classes evidenced a fundamental social change and a great threat to traditional modes of deference; and, finally, perhaps, a recognition of the restrictive nature of that deference society registered precisely in the continous fascination for the disorderly other.

The thrust into Ireland from the 1530s sought to consolidate and expand British political control and economic exploitation of a strategic marginal area previously only partially under British authority. D. B. Quinn has shown that the major policies of this expansion included plantation of British settlements in key areas, the establishment of a docile landed elite, the fossilisation of the social order in areas under British control, the conversion of Gaelic customs into their "civil" counterparts and the introduction of English as the sole official language. These policies were exercised partly through a vast discursive production of Ireland and the Irish. The virtuous and vicious potentialities that were attributed to Pocahontas predominate in such discourse. Ireland was therefore a savage land that might yet be made to flow with milk and honey like a new Canaan. Similarly the Irish were seen as both savage Gaels and lapsed civil subjects. This arose out of historic claims that the land was *both* a feudal fief under British lordship (then, under the Tudors, under direct British sovereignty), whose truant subjects needed reordering and pacification *and* also a colony, where the savage other needed to be civilised, conquered, dispossessed. The discourse afforded a flexible ensemble to be mobilised in the service of the varying fortune of the British in their semiperiphery.

In this highly complex discourse an "elementary ethnology" was formulated in which the various cultures of Ireland might be examined, and evidence gathered to show their inferiority to civility even as their potential for exploitation was assessed. As with the Negro or Amerindian, the Irish might be constituted as bestial or only marginally human and, as such, totally irreformable. For example, in 1594 Dawtrey drew upon a whole stock of commonplaces to give his opinion of the possibility of change in the Irish: "an ape will be an ape though he were clad in cloth of gold." It should be noted that Stephano's and Trinculo's masterless aping of the aristocrats in 4.1, where they steal rich clothes off a line, bears the weight of this stereotypicality—and their subsequent punishment, being hunted with dogs, draws full attention to their bestiality.

Even if granted human status, Gaelic modes of social behaviour were viewed as the antithesis of civil codes. In Spenser's account of booleying (the seasonal migration of livestock and owners to summer pasture), this wandering and unsupervised operation enables its practioners to "grow thereby the more barbarous and live more licentiously than they could in towns, . . . for there they think themselves half exempted from law and obedience, and having once tasted freedom do, like a steer that hath long been out of his yoke, grudge and repine ever after to come under rule again" ("A View of The Present State of Ireland" [1596]). Barbarity is opposed to the life of the town or *polis,* and the booleyers evade the law, conferring upon themselves the status of truants or outlaws—masterless men. Each social relegation marks the Irish off again as beast-like, requiring the management of the British husbandman.

Within this general delineation of masterless barbarity, particular classes of footloose Irish were specifically targeted, especially jesters (again notice how Trinculo is related to such exemplary antitypes), "carrows" (or gamblers), wolvine "kernes" (or foot soldiers) and bards. Such figures literally embodied the masterless / savage threat and their suppression became a symbolic statement of British intent for the whole of uncivil Ireland.

More positive versions of Ireland were also produced, particularly in those texts which advocated plantation of the English beyond the Pale. Such versions produce Irish culture, generally, along the lines of a "negative formula," in which the alien is afforded no positive terms but merely displays the absence of those qualities that connote civility, for example, no law, no government, no marriage, no social hierarchy, no visible mode of production, no permanent settlement. Again *The Tempest* is implicated in such a strategy. Gonzalo's description of his imagined island kingdom in 2.1, culled from Montaigne, rehearses the standard formula by which the colonised is denigrated even as it appears to be simply the idle thoughts of a stranded courtier.

At its most optimistic the negative formula represents the other as a natural simplicity against which a jaded civility might be criticised, yet even here the other is produced for the use of civility, to gauge *its* present crisis. Nevertheless, the other's critical function must not be overlooked, as I hope to demonstrate with *The Tempest.* The more typical orientation of the other around the negative formula, however, is the production of a tabula rasa. Eden's translation of Peter Martyr's *Decades* (1555) provides a central statement of such a strategy. The Amerindians are "Gentiles" who "may well be likened to a smooth, bare table unpainted, or a white paper unwritten, upon the which you may at the first paint or write what you list, as you cannot upon tables already painted, unless you raze or blot out the first forms." Here the other is an empty space to be inscribed at will by the desire of the coloniser. In some accounts of Ireland the land and the bulk of its peasantry were this unpainted table. Yet contradictorily, for instance in the version of Sir John Davies, before it could be painted at will certain obdurate forms, tyrannical lords and customs had to be razed.

So vacuous or vicious, docile or destructive, such stereotypical production announced the triumph of civility or declared the other's usefulness for its purposes. But a dark countertruth needed to be acknowledged. The inferior culture of the Gaels had absorbed the Old English invaders, as Davies noted with horror: "The English, who hoped to make a perfect conquest of the Irish, were by them perfectly and absolutely conquered" ("A Discovery of The True Causes Why Ireland Was Never Subdued . . . Until The Beginning of His Majesty's Happy Reign"). The possibility of "going native" was constantly evidenced in this example, which Davies likened to the vicious transformation of Nebudchadnezzar or the Circean swine. The supposed *binary* division of civil and other into virtue/vice, positive/negative, etc, was shown to be erodable as the forces of the subordinate term of the opposition seeped back into the privileged term. The blank spaces of Ireland provided not only an opportunity for the expansion of civility; they were also sites for the possible undoing of civil man, offering a "freedom" (Spenser's term for the avoidance of civility in the quotation above) in which he might lapse into masterlessness and savagism. The same discourse which allows for the transformation of the savage into the civil also raises the possibility of a reverse transformation. As Davies could announce a hope for the homogenisation of the Irish into civility "so that we may conceive an hope that the next generation will in tongue and heart and every way else become English," so Spenser could remark of civil man: "Lord, how quickly doth that country alter men's natures."

Given the importance of the colonisation of Ireland for British expansionism, together with its complex discursive formation which I have outlined briefly, it is surprising that such scant attention has been paid to such material in relation to *The Tempest*. I am not suggesting that Irish colonial discourse should be ransacked to find possible sources for some of the play's phraseology. Rather (as Hulme and Barker suggest) we should note a general analogy between text and context; specifically, between Ireland and Prospero's island. They are both marginally situated in semiperipheral areas (Ireland is geographically semiperipheral, its subjects both truant civilians and savages, as Prospero's island is ambiguously placed between American and European discourse). Both places are described as "uninhabited" (that is, connoting the absence of civility) and yet are peopled with a strange admixture of the savage and masterless other, powerfully controlling and malcontentedly lapsed civil subjects. Both locations are subject to powerful organising narratives which recount the beleaguerments, loss and recovery—the ravelling and unravelling—of colonising subjects. Such discourse provides the richest and the most fraught discussion of colonialism at the moment of the play's inception.

Much of my analysis above has been theoretically informed by Edward Said's account of orientalist discourse. Orientalism is not simply a discourse which produces a certain knowledge of the East, rather it is a "western style for dominating, restructuring and having authority over the Orient" (*Orientalism*). Although it cannot be simply correlated with the process of *material* exploitation of the East, the discourse produces a form of knowledge which is of great utility in aiding this process—serving to define the West as its origin, serving to relegate alien cultures, serving even the voyeuristic and libidinal desire of the western man who is denied such expression elsewhere.

Homi K. Bhabha's recent account of the colonialist stereotype effects a critique of Said, suggesting that even in the stereotype there is something which prevents it from being *totally* useful for the coloniser. Bhabha says the stereotype "connotes rigidity and an unchanging order as well as disorder, degeneracy and demonic repetition" ("The Other Question," *Screen* 24 [1983]). This is to say that at the heart of the stereotype, a discursive strategy designed to locate or "fix" a colonial other in a position of inferiority to the coloniser, the potentiality of a disruptive threat must be admitted. For example, if a stereotype declares the black to be rapacious, then even as it marks him as inferior to the self-controlled white, it announces his power to violate, and thus requires the imposition of restraint if such power is to be curtailed: so the stereotype cannot rest, it is always impelled to *further* action.

To summarise, I have begun to suggest that colonialist discourse voices a demand both for order and disorder, producing a disruptive other in order to assert the superiority of the coloniser. Yet that production is itself evidence of a struggle to restrict the other's disruptiveness to that role. Colonialist discourse does not simply announce a triumph for civility, it must continually *produce* it, and this work involves struggle and risk. It is this complex relation between the intention to produce colonialist stereotypicality, its beleaguerments and even its possible erosion in the face of the other that I now wish to trace through *The Tempest*.

The play begins in an apparent disruption of that social deference and elemental harmony which characterise the representation of courtly authority in Renaissance dramaturgy. Yet this initial "tempest" becomes retroactively a kind of antimasque or disorderly prelude to the assertion of that courtly authority which was supposedly in jeopardy. From Prospero's initial appearance it becomes clear that disruption was produced to create a series of problems precisely in order to effect their resolution. The dramatic conflict of the opening of the play is to be reordered to declare the mastery of Prospero in being able to initiate and control such dislocation and dispersal. This narrative intention is a correlate of the courtly masque proper, in which, conflict having been eradicated, elaborate and declarative compliment might be made to the supervising sovereign (as in the Hombre Salvagio episode, above). Prospero's problems concerning the maintenance of his power on the island are therefore also problems of representation, of his capacity to "forge" the island in his own image. The production of narrative, in this play, is always related to questions of power.

In his powerful narrative, Prospero interpellates the various listeners— calls to them, as it were, and invites them to recognise themselves as subjects of his discourse, as beneficiaries of his civil largesse. Thus for Miranda he is a strong father who educates and protects her; for Ariel he is a rescuer and taskmaster; for Caliban he is a coloniser whose refused offer of civilisation forces him to strict discipline; for the shipwrecked he is a surrogate providence who corrects errant aristocrats and punishes plebeian revolt. Each of these subject positions confirms Prospero as master.

The second scene of the play is an extended demonstration of Prospero's powerful narration as it interpellates Miranda, Ariel and Caliban. It is recounted as something importantly rescued out of the "dark backward and abysm of time" (1.2.50), a remembrance of things past soon revealed as a mnemonic of power. This is to say, Prospero's narrative demands of its subjects that they should accede to *his* version of the past. For Miranda, Prospero's account of her origins is a tale of the neglect of office, leading to a fraternal usurpation and a banishment, followed by a miraculous landfall on the island. Prospero first tells of his loss of civil power and then of its renewal, in magic, upon the marginal space of the island. This reinvestiture in civil power through the medium of the non-civil is an essentially colonialist discourse. However, the narrative is fraught because it reveals internal contradictions which strain its ostensible project and because it produces the possibility of sites of resistance in the other precisely at the moment when it seeks to impose its captivating power.

In the recitation to Miranda, for example, Prospero is forced to remember his own past *forgetfulness,* since it was his devotion to private study that allowed his unsupervised brother, masterlessly, to seize power. He is forced to recall a division between liberal and stately arts which are ideally united in the princely magus of masquing fiction. However as the recitation continues, this essentially political disjunction becomes simply the pretext or initial disruption that is replaced by a mysterious account of the recovery of civil power, the reunification of the liberal artist and the politic sovereign. It is re-presented as a *felix culpa,* a fortunate fall, in which court intrigue becomes reinscribed in the terms of romance, via a shift from the language of courtiership to that of courtship, to a rhetoric of love and charity.

This is marked by a series of tropes deriving from courtly love conventions, as Kermode notes. The deposed duke becomes a helpless exile who cries into the sea, which charitably responds, as does the wind, with pity (ll. 148–50). The deposition becomes a "loving wrong" (l. 151)—again the very form of oxymoron is typical of Petrarchan love sonnetry. These romance tropes effect a transition from a discourse of power to one of powerlessness. This mystifies the origin of what is after all a colonialist regime on the island by producing it as the result of charitable acts (by the sea, the wind and the honest courtier, Gonzalo, alike) made out of pity for powerless exiles. Recent important work on pastoral and amatory sonnet sequences has shown how such a rhetoric of love, charity and romance is always already involved in the mediation of power relations. Prospero's mystifying narrative here has precisely these effects. Further, his scheme for the resumption of his dukedom and his reintegration with the larger political world is also inscribed in such terms, as a courtship of "bountiful Fortune," his "dear lady," or of an auspicious star which "If now I court her not, but omit, my fortunes / Will ever after droop" (see ll. 179–84). And, of course, a major strategy of this scheme is to engineer another courtship, between Miranda and the son of his old enemy—his daughter having been duly educated for such a role in the enclosed and enchanted space of the island. The entire production of the island here, ostensibly an escape or exile from the world of statism, is thoroughly instrumental, even if predicated upon an initial loss of power.

In the same scene Prospero reminds Ariel of his indebtedness to the master, an act of memory which it is necessary to repeat monthly (ll. 261–63). This constant reminding operates as a mode of "symbolic violence": What is really at issue is the underlining of a power relation. Ariel is, paradoxically, *bound* in service by this constant reminder of Prospero's gift of *freedom* to him, in releasing him from imprisonment in a tree. That bondage is reinforced by both a promise to repeat the act of release when a period of servitude has expired and a promise to repeat the act of incarceration should service not be forthcoming. In order to do this, Prospero utilises the previous regime of Sycorax as an evil other. Her black, female magic ostensibly contrasts with that of Prospero in that it is remembered as viciously coercive, yet beneath the apparent voluntarism of the white, male regime lies the threat of precisely this coercion. This tends to produce an identification between the regimes, which is underscored by biographical similarities such as that both rulers are magicians, both have been exiled because of their practices, both have nurtured children on the isle. The most apparent distinction between black and white regimes would seem to be that the latter is simply more powerful and more flexible. Part of its flexibility is its capacity to produce and utilise an other in order to obtain the consent of Ariel to his continued subjugation.

Caliban, on the other hand, is nakedly enslaved to the master. The narrative of 1.2 legitimises this exercise of power by representing Caliban's resistance to colonisation as the obdurate and irresponsible refusal of a simple educative project. This other, the offspring of a witch and a devil, the wild man and savage, the emblem of morphological ambivalence (see Hulme, "Hurricans in the Caribees"), was even without language before the arrival of the exiles. It was Miranda, the civil virgin, who, out of pity, taught Caliban to "know thine own meaning" (ll. 358). Yet, as with the Hombre Salvagio above, the "gift" of language also inscribes a power relation as the other is hailed and recognises himself as a linguistic subject of the master language. Caliban's refusal marks him as obdurate yet he must voice this in a curse in the language of civility, representing himself as a subject of what he so accurately describes as "*your* language" (l. 367, my stress). Whatever Caliban does with this gift announces his capture by it.

Yet within the parameters of this capture Caliban is able to create a resistance. Ostensibly *produced* as an other to provide the pretext for the exercise of naked power, he is also a *producer,* provoking reaction in the master. He does not come when called, which makes Prospero angry (ll. 315–22). Then he greets the colonisers with a curse, provoking the master to curse in reply, reducing the eloquent master of civil language to the raucous registers of the other (ll. 323–32). Third, he ignores the civil curse and proceeds with his own narrative, in which Prospero himself is designated as usurping other to Caliban's initial monarchy and hospitality (ll. 333–46). Such discursive strategies show that Caliban has indeed mastered enough of the lessons of civility to ensure that its interpellation of him as simply savage, "a born devil, on whose nature / Nurture can never stick" (4.1.188–89), is inadequate. Paradoxically, it is the eloquent power of civility which allows him to know his *own* meaning, offering him a site of resistance even as civility's coercive capacities finally reduce him to silence (ll. 373–75).

The island itself is an "uninhabited" spot, a tabula rasa peopled fortuitously by the shipwrecked. Two children, Miranda and Caliban, have been nurtured upon it. Prospero's narrative operates to produce in them the binary division of the other, into the malleable and the irreformable, that I have shown to be a major strategy of colonialist discourse. There is

Miranda, miraculous courtly lady, virgin prospect (cf. Virginia itself) and there is Caliban, scrambled "cannibal," savage incarnate. Presiding over them is the cabalist Prospero, whose function it is to divide and demarcate these potentialities, arrogating to the male all that is debased and rapacious, to the female all that is cultured and needs protection.

Such a division of the "children" is validated in Prospero's narrative by the memory of Caliban's attempted rape of Miranda (1.2.347–53), which immediately follows Caliban's own account of his boundless hospitality to the exiles on their arrival (ll. 333–46). The issue here is not whether Caliban is actually a rapist or not, since Caliban accepts the charge. I am rather concerned with the political effects of this charge at this moment in the play. The first effect is to circumvent Caliban's version of events by reencoding his boundlessness as rapacity: his inability to discern a concept of private, bounded property concerning his own dominions is reinterpreted as a desire to violate the chaste virgin, who epitomises courtly property. Second, the capacity to divide and order is shown to be the prerogative of the courtly ruler alone. Third, the memory legitimises Prospero's takeover of power.

Such a sexual division of the other into rapist and virgin is common in colonialist discourse. In *The Faerie Queene,* for example, Ireland is presented as both Irene, a courtly virgin, and Grantorto, a rapacious woodkerne from whom the virgin requires protection, thus validating the intervention of the British knight, Artegall, and his killing machine, Talus. Similarly, in Purchas's *Virginia's Verger* of 1625 the uprising of 1622 is shown to be an act of incestuous rape by native sons upon a virgin land, and this declares the rightfulness of the betrothal of that land to duly respectful civil husbandmen, engaged in "presenting her as a chaste virgin to Christ" (see Porter, *The Inconstant Savage*). Miranda is represented as just such a virgin, to be protected from the rapist native and presented to a civil lover, Ferdinand. The "fatherly" power of the coloniser, and his capacity to regulate and utilise the sexuality of his subject "children," is therefore a potent trope as activated in the *The Tempest* and again demonstrates the crucial nexus of civil power and sexuality in colonial discourse. The other is here presented to legitimate the seizure of power by civility and to define by antithesis (rape) the proper course of civil courtship—a channelling of desire into a series of formal tasks and manoeuvres and, finally, into courtly marriage. Such a virtuous consummation is predicated upon the disruptive potential of carnality, embodied in the rapist other and in the potentially truant desires of the courtly lovers themselves, which Prospero constantly warns them against (as at 4.1.15–23 and 51–54). With little evidence of such truancy,

Prospero's repeated warnings reassert his power to regulate sexuality just at the point when such regulatory power is being transferred from father to husband. Yet his continued insistence on the power of desire to disrupt courtly form surely also evidences an unease, an anxiety, about the power of civility to deliver control over a force which it locates both in the other and in the civil subject.

A capacity to divide and demarcate groups of subjects along class lines is also demonstrated. The shipwrecked courtiers are dispersed on the island into two groups, aristocrats and plebians. The usurping "men of sin" in the courtly group are first maddened, then recuperated; the drunken servants, unmastered, are simply punished and held up to ridicule. This division of masterless behaviour serves a complex hegemonic function: the unselfmastered aristocrats are reabsorbed, after correction, into the governing class, their new solidarity underscored by their collective laughter at the chastened revolting plebians. The class joke acts as a recuperative and defusive strategy which celebrates the renewal of courtly hegemony and displaces its breakdown on to the ludicrous revolt of the masterless.

Such binarism is also apparent in productions such as Ben Jonson's *Irish Masque at Court* (first put on in December 1613). Here indecorous stage-Irish plebeians are banished from the royal presence, to be replaced with the courtly exemplars of newly converted Anglo-Irish civility. In this James I's coercive power is celebrated as music. Now Ireland has stooped to "the music of his peace, / She need not with the spheres change harmony." This harmonics of power causes the Irish aristocrats to slough off their former dress and customs to emerge as English court butterflies; the ant-like rabble are precluded from such a metamorphosis.

This last example demonstrates another strategy by which sovereign power might at once be praised and effaced *as power* in colonialist discourse. In this masque, power is represented as an *aesthetic* ordering. This correlates with Prospero's investment in the power of narrative to maintain social control and with *The Tempest*'s production of the origins of colonialism through the rhetoric of romance, its representation of colonial power as a gift of freedom or of education, its demonstration of colonialist organisation as a "family romance" involving the management and reordering of disruptive desire. The play's observation of the classical unities (of space, time and action), its use of harmonious music to lead, enchant, relax, restore, its constant reference to the leisured space of pastoral and the dream, all underline this aesthetic and disinterested, harmonious and nonexploitative representation of power. In a sermon of Richard Crashaw (1610), the latent mechanisms of power which actually promote the metamorphosis of jaded civil subjects is acknowledged: the transplanted, if "subject to some pinching miseries and to a strict form of government and severe discipline, do often become new men, even as it were cast in a new mould." *The Tempest* is, therefore, fully implicated in the process of "euphemisation," the effacement of power—yet, as I have begun to demonstrate, the play also reveals precisely "the strict form of government" which actually underpins the miraculous narrative of "sea change." The play oscillates uneasily between mystification and revelation and this is crucially demonstrated in the presentation of the plebeian revolt.

The process of euphemisation depends upon the rebellious misalliance of Caliban and Stephano and Trinculo being recognised as a kind of antimasque, yet there are features of this representation which disrupt such a recognition. Ostensibly the "low" scenes of the play ape courtly actions and demonstrate the latter's superiority. The initial encounter of the masterless and the savage, for example, is analogous to the encounter between the civil and the savage narrated by Prospero, and to the encounter of the New World virgin and the gallant courtier enacted before the audience. Caliban's hospitality to Prospero is repeated as an act of voluntary subjection to the actually powerless exile, Stephano. This act is a bathetic version of the idealised meeting of civil and savage epitomised in the Hombre Salvagio episode—Caliban misrecognises *true* sovereignty and gives his fealty rather to a drunken servant. Unlike the immediate recognition of a common courtly bond which Miranda and Ferdinand experience, the savage and the masterless reveal a spontaneous *non-civil* affinity. More locally, as the courtly exiles brought Caliban the gift of language, so the masterless donate "that which will give language to you, cat,"—a bottle (2.2.84–85); the former imposes linguistic capture and restraint, the latter offers release.

Yet the issue is more complex, for what this misalliance mediates, in "low" terms, is precisely a colonising situation. Only here can the colonising process be viewed as nakedly avaricious, profiteering, perhaps even pointless (the expense of effort to no end rather than a proper teleological civil investment). Stephano, for example, contemplates taming and exhibiting Caliban for gain (2.2.78–80). Also, the masterless do not lead but are led around by the savage, who must constantly remind them of their rebellious plans (see 4.1.231–32). This low version of colonialism serves to displace possibly damaging charges which might be levied against properly constituted civil authority on to the already excremental products of civility, the masterless. This allows those charges to be announced and defused, transforming a possible anxiety into pleasure at the ludicrous antics of the low who will, after all, be punished in due course.

This analysis still produces the other as being in the (complex) service of civility, even if the last paragraph suggests that a possible anxiety is being displaced. Yet there is a manifest contradiction in the representation of the misalliance which I have not considered so far: in denigrating the masterless, such scenes foreground more positive qualities in the savage. The banter of the drunkards serves to counterpoint moments of great eloquence in the obdurate slave. Amid all the comic business, Caliban describes the effects of the island music:

> the isle is full of noises,
> Sounds and sweet airs, that give delight, and hurt not.
> Sometimes a thousand twangling instruments
> Will hum about mine ears; and sometimes voices,
> That, if I then had wak'd after long sleep,
> Will make me sleep again: and then, in dreaming,
> The clouds methought would open, and show riches
> Ready to drop upon me: that, when I wak'd,
> I cried to dream again.
>
> (3.2.133–41)

Here the island is seen to operate not for the coloniser but for the colonised. Prospero utilises music to charm, punish and restore his various subjects, employing it like James I in a harmonics of power. For Caliban, music provokes a dream wish for the riches which in reality are denied him by colonising power. There seems to be a quality in the island beyond the requirements of the coloniser's powerful harmonics, a quality existing for itself, which the other may use to resist, if only in dream, the repressive reality which hails him as villain—both a feudalised bonded workhorse and evil incarnate.

This production of a site beyond colonial appropriation can only be represented through colonialist discourse, however, since Caliban's eloquence is after all "your language," the language of the coloniser. Obviously the play itself, heavily invested in colonialist discourse, can only represent this moment of excess through that very discourse: and so the discourse itself may be said to produce this site of resistance. Yet what precisely is at stake here?

The answer I believe is scandalously simple. Caliban's dream is not the *antithesis* but the *apotheosis* of colonialist discourse. If this discourse seeks to efface its own power, then here at last is an eloquent spokesman who is powerless; here such eloquence represents not a desire to control and rule but a fervent wish for release, a desire to escape reality and return to dream.

Caliban's production of the island as a pastoral space, separated from the world of power, takes *literally* what the discourse in the hands of a Prospero can only mean *metaphorically*. This is to say, the colonialist project's investment in the processes of euphemisation of what are really powerful relations here has produced a utopian moment where powerlessness represents *a desire for powerlessness*. This is the danger that any metaphorical system faces, that vehicle may be taken for tenor and used against the ostensible meanings intended. The play registers, if only momentarily, a radical ambivalence at the heart of colonialist discourse, revealing that it is a site of *struggle* over meaning.

Prospero's narrative can be seen, then, to operate as a reality principle, ordering and correcting the inhabitants of the island, subordinating their discourse to his own. A more potent metaphor, however, might be the concept of dreamwork—that labour undertaken to represent seamlessly and palatably what in reality is a contest between a censorship and a latent drive. The masterful operations of censorship are apparent everywhere in *The Tempest*. In the terminology of the analysis of dreamwork developed by Freud, these political operations may be discerned as displacement (for example, the displacement of the fear of noble insurrection on to the easily defeated misalliance), condensation (the condensation of the whole colonial project into the terms of a patriarchal demarcation of sexuality), symbolisation (the emblems of the vanishing banquet, the marriage masque, the discovery of the lovers at chess) and secondary revision (the ravelling up of the narrative dispersal of the storm scene, the imposition of Prospero's memory over that of his subjects, etc.). As I have attempted to show above with specific examples, such operations encode struggle and contradiction even as they, or *because* they, strive to insist on the legitimacy of colonialist narrative.

Further, as this narrative progresses, its master appears more and more to divest himself of the very power he has so relentlessly sought. As Fiedler brilliantly notes, in the courtship game in which Miranda is a pawn, even as Prospero's gameplan succeeds he himself is played out, left without a move as power over his daughter slips away. So the magus abjures his magic, his major source of coercive power (5.1.33–57). This is ostensibly replaced by civil power as Prospero resorts to his "hat and rapier," twin markers of the governor (the undoffed hat signifying a high status in a deference society, as the rapier signifies the aristocratic right to carry such weaponry). Yet this resumption of power entails the relinquishing of revenge upon the usurpers, an end to the exploitation and punishment of the masterless and the savage, even an exile from the island. Further, he goes home not to resume public duty but to retire and think of death (see 5.1.310–11). The completion of the colonialist project signals the banishment of its supreme exponent even as his triumph is declared.

Is this final distancing of the master from his narrative an unravelling of his project? Or is this displacement merely the final example of that courtly euphemisation of power outlined above? One last example must serve to demonstrate that the "ending" of the play is in fact a struggle between the apotheosis and the aporia of colonialist discourse. The marriage masque of 4.1 demonstrates Prospero's capacity to order native spirits to perform a courtly narrative of his own design. In addition, this production is consented to by the audience of the two courtly lovers, whose pleasure itself shows that they are bound by the narrative. As such, the masque is a model of ideological interpellation, securing chastity, a state which the master continually *demands* of the lovers, through active consent rather than coercive power. Further, Prospero's instructions to his audience before the masque begins implicitly rehearse his ideal subject-audience: "No tongue! All eyes! be silent" (4.1.59). Yet the masque is disrupted, as Prospero is drawn back from this moment of the declaration of his triumph into the realm of struggle, for Caliban's plot must be dealt with. Although the plot is allowed for in his timetable (see 4.1.141–42) and is demonstrably ineffectual, this irruption of the antimasque into the masque proper has a totally disproportionate effect to its actual capacity to seize power. The masque is dispelled and Prospero utters a monologue upon the illusory nature of all representation, even of the world itself (4.1.153–58). Hitherto he has insisted that his narrative be taken as real and powerful—now it is collapsed, along with everything else, into the "stuff" of dreams. The forging of colonialist narrative is, momentarily, revealed as a forgery. Yet, Prospero goes on to meet the threat and triumph over it, thus completing his narrative. What is profoundly ambivalent here is the relation between narrative declaration and dramatic struggle. Prospero requires a struggle with the forces of the other in order to show his power: struggle is therefore the precondition for the announcement of his victory. Yet here the moment of declaration is disrupted as a further contest arises: Prospero must repeat the process of struggle. It is *he* who largely produces the ineffectual challenge as a dire threat. This is to say, the colonialist narrative requires and produces the other—another which continually destabilises and disperses the narrative's moment of conviction. The threat must be present to validate colonialist discourse; yet if present it cannot but impel the narrative to further action. The process is interminable. Yet the play has to end.

Given this central ambivalence in the narrative, and given Prospero's problematic relationship to the restitution of civil power, it falls upon the honest old courtier, Gonzalo, actually to announce the closure of the narrative. He confirms that all is restored, including "all of us ourselves / When no man was his own" (see 5.1.206–13). True civil subjectivity is declared: the encounter with the forces of otherness on the island produces a signal victory. Yet the architect of that victory is to retire and die, his narrative a mere entertainment to while away the last night on the isle, his actor reduced in the epilogue to beg for the release of applause. When apportioning the plebeians to the masters, he assigns Caliban to himself, saying "this thing of darkness I / Acknowledge mine" (5.1.275–76). Even as this powerfully designates the monster as his property, an object for his own utility, a darkness from which he may rescue self-knowledge, there is surely an ironic identification *with* the other here as both become interstitial. Only a displacement of the narrating function from the master to a simpler, declarative civilian courtier can hope to terminate the endless struggle to relate self and other so as to serve the colonialist project. At the "close" of the play, Prospero is in danger of becoming the other to the narrative declaration of his own project, which is precisely the ambivalent position Caliban occupies.

The Tempest, then, declares no all-embracing triumph for colonialism. Rather it serves as a limit text in which the characteristic operations of colonialist discourse may be discerned—as an instrument of exploitation, a register of beleaguerment and a site of radical ambivalence. These operations produce strategies and stereotypes which seek to impose and efface colonialist power; in this text they are also driven into contradiction and disruption. The play's "ending" in renunciation and restoration is only the final ambivalence, being at once the apotheosis, mystification and potential erosion of the colonialist discourse. If this powerful discourse, thus mediated, is finally reduced to the stuff of dreams, then it is still dreamwork, the site of a struggle for meaning. My project has been to attempt a repunctuation of the play so that it may reveal its involvement in colonial practices, speak something of the ideological contradictions of its *political* unconscious.

Chronology

1564	William Shakespeare born at Stratford-on-Avon to John Shakespeare, a butcher, and Mary Arden. He is baptized on April 26.
1582	Marries Anne Hathaway in November.
1583	Daughter Susanna born, baptized on May 26.
1585	Twins Hamnet and Judith born, baptized on February 2.
1588–90	Sometime during these years, Shakespeare goes to London, without family. First plays performed in London.
1590–92	*The Comedy of Errors*, the three parts of *Henry VI*.
1593–94	Publication of *Venus and Adonis* and *The Rape of Lucrece*, both dedicated to the Earl of Southampton. Shakespeare becomes a sharer in the Lord Chamberlain's company of actors. *The Taming of the Shrew*, *The Two Gentlemen of Verona*, *Richard III*, *Titus Andronicus*.
1595–97	*Romeo and Juliet*, *Richard II*, *King John*, *A Midsummer Night's Dream*, *Love's Labor's Lost*.
1596	Son Hamnet dies. Grant of arms to Shakespeare's father.
1597	*The Merchant of Venice*, *Henry IV*, *Part 1*. Purchases New Place in Stratford.
1598–1600	*Henry IV*, *Part 2*, *As You Like It*, *Much Ado about Nothing*, *Twelfth Night*, *The Merry Wives of Windsor*, *Henry V*, and *Julius Caesar*. Moves his company to the new Globe Theatre.
1601	*Hamlet*. Shakespeare's father dies, buried on September 8.
1601–2	*Troilus and Cressida*.
1603	Death of Queen Elizabeth; James VI of Scotland becomes James I of England; Shakespeare's company becomes the King's Men.
1603–4	*All's Well That Ends Well*, *Measure for Measure*, *Othello*.

Contributors

HAROLD BLOOM, Sterling Professor of the Humanities at Yale University, is the author of *The Anxiety of Influence, Poetry and Repression,* and many other volumes of literary criticism. His forthcoming study, *Freud: Transference and Authority,* attempts a full-scale reading of all of Freud's major writings. A MacArthur Prize Fellow, he is general editor of five series of literary criticism published by Chelsea House. During 1987-88, he served as the Charles Eliot Norton Professor of Poetry at Harvard University.

HARRY BERGER, JR., is Professor of English at Cowell College at the University of California, Santa Cruz. He is the author of *The Allegorical Temper.*

MARJORIE GARBER is Professor of English at Harvard University. She is the author of many articles on Shakespeare, Marlowe, and Milton in addition to *Dream in Shakespeare: From Metaphor to Metamorphosis* and *Coming of Age in Shakespeare,* a study of maturation patterns and rites of passage in the plays.

STEPHEN J. GREENBLATT is Professor of English at the University of California, Berkeley. His works include *Sir Walter Raleigh: The Renaissance Man and His Roles* and *Renaissance Self-Fashioning: From More to Shakespeare.*

JULIAN PATRICK is Professor of English at Victoria College, University of Toronto. He is coeditor of *Centre and Labyrinth: Essays in Honour of Northrop Frye.*

JAMES P. DRISCOLL is the author of *Identity in Shakespearean Drama.*

STEPHEN ORGEL is Professor of English at Stanford University. He is the author of *The Jonsonian Masque* and *The Illusion of Power.* He has also edited the complete poems of Christopher Marlowe and numerous anthologies of literary criticism.

BARBARA HOWARD TRAISTER is Professor of English at Lehigh University. She is the author of *Heavenly Necromancers: The Magician in English Renaissance Drama*.

PAUL BROWN has published on Shakespeare.

Bibliography

Abrams, Richard. "*The Tempest* and the Concept of the Machiavellian Playwright." *English Literary Renaissance* 8 (1978): 43–66.

Allman, Eileen Jorge. *Player-King and Adversary: Two Faces of Play in Shakespeare*. Baton Rouge: Louisiana State University Press, 1980.

Aronson, Alex. *Psyche and Symbol in Shakespeare*. Bloomington: Indiana University Press, 1972.

Arthos, John. *Shakespeare's Use of Dream and Vision*. London: Bowes & Bowes, 1977.

Bamber, Linda. *Comic Women, Tragic Men: A Study of Gender and Genre in Shakespeare*. Stanford: Stanford University Press, 1982.

Barker, Francis, and Peter Hulme. "Nymphs and Reapers Heavily Vanish: The Discursive Con-texts of *The Tempest*." In *Alternative Shakespeares*, edited by John Drakakis, 191–205. London: Methuen, 1985.

Berger, Karol. "Prospero's Art." *Shakespeare Studies* 10 (1977): 211–39.

Bergeron, David M. *Shakespeare's Romances and the Royal Family*. Lawrence: University Press of Kansas, 1985.

———. "The Tempest/*The Tempest*." *Essays in Literature* 7 (1980): 3–9.

Berry, Ralph. *The Shakespearean Metaphor: Studies in Language and Form*. London: Macmillan, 1978.

Bradbrook, M. C. "Shakespeare's Primitive Art." *Proceedings of the British Academy* 51 (1965): 215–34.

Brailow, David C. "Prospero's 'Old Brain': The Old Man as Metaphor in *The Tempest*." *Shakespeare Survey* 14 (1981): 285–303.

Brockbank, Philip. "*The Tempest:* Conventions of Art and Empire." In *Later Shakespeare,* edited by John Russell Brown and Bernard Harris, 183–201. Stratford-Upon-Avon Studies, no. 8. New York: St. Martin's, 1967.

Brower, Reuben A. *The Fields of Light: An Experiment in Critical Reading*. New York: Oxford University Press, 1951.

Brown, John Russell. *Shakespeare and His Comedies*. London: Methuen, 1957.

Bryant, J. A., Jr. *Shakespeare and the Uses of Comedy*. Lexington: University Press of Kentucky, 1986.

Bullough, Geoffrey, ed. *Narrative and Dramatic Sources of Shakespeare, Vol. 8: Romances*. London: Routledge & Kegan Paul, 1975.

Cantor, Paul A. "Prospero's Republic: The Politics of Shakespeare's *The Tempest*."

In *Shakespeare as a Political Thinker*, edited by John Alvis and Thomas G. West, 239–55. Durham, N.C.: Carolina Academic Press, 1981.

———. "Shakespeare's *The Tempest*: The Wise Man as Hero." *Shakespeare Quarterly* 31 (1980): 64–75.

Carroll, William C. *The Metamorphosis of Shakespearean Comedy*. Princeton, N.J.: Princeton University Press, 1985.

Cobb, Noel. *Prospero's Island: The Secret Alchemy at the Heart of* The Tempest. London: Coventure, 1984.

Comito, Terry. "Caliban's Dream: The Topography of Some Shakespeare Gardens." *Shakespeare Studies* 14 (1981): 23–54.

Corfield, Cosmo. "Why Does Prospero Abjure His 'Rough Magic'?" *Shakespeare Quarterly* 36 (1985): 31–48.

Coursen, Herbert R., Jr. "Prospero and the Drama of the Soul." *Shakespeare Studies* 4 (1968): 316–33.

Craig, Hardin. "Magic in *The Tempest*." *Philological Quarterly* 47 (1968): 8-15.

Curry, Walter Clyde. *Shakespeare's Philosophical Patterns*. Baton Rouge: Louisiana State University Press, 1937.

Davies, Stevie. *The Feminine Reclaimed: The Idea of Woman in Spenser, Shakespeare, and Milton*. Lexington: University Press of Kentucky, 1986.

Dawson, Anthony B. *Indirections: Shakespeare and the Art of Illusion*. Toronto: University of Toronto Press, 1978.

Dean, John. *Restless Wanderers: Shakespeare and the Pattern of Romance*. Atlantic Highlands, N.J.: Humanities Press, 1979.

de Grazia, Margareta. "*The Tempest*: Gratuitous Movement, or Action without Kibes and Pinches." *Shakespeare Studies* 14 (1981): 249–65.

Dobrée, Bonamy. "*The Tempest*." In *Shakespeare: The Comedies: A Collection of Critical Essays,* edited by Kenneth Muir, 164–75. Englewood Cliffs, N.J.: Prentice-Hall, 1965.

Doran, Madeleine. *Endeavors of Art: A Study of Form in Elizabethan Art*. Madison: University of Wisconsin Press, 1954.

Dreher, Diane Elizabeth. *Domination and Defiance: Fathers and Daughters in Shakespeare*. Lexington: University Press of Kentucky, 1986.

Eagleton, Terry. *Shakespeare and Society: Critical Studies in Shakespearean Drama*. New York: Schocken, 1967.

———. *William Shakespeare*. New York: Oxford University Press, 1986.

Ebner, Dean. "*The Tempest*: Rebellion and the Ideal State." *Shakespeare Quarterly* 16 (1965): 161–73.

Edwards, Philip. *Shakespeare and the Confines of Art*. London: Methuen, 1968.

Egan, Robert. *Drama within Drama: Shakespeare's Sense of His Art in* King Lear, The Winter's Tale, *and* The Tempest. New York: Columbia University Press, 1975.

Eggers, Walter F., Jr. "Bring Forth a Wonder: Presentation in Shakespeare's Romances." *Texas Studies in Literature and Language* 21 (Winter 1979): 455–77.

Epstein, Harry. "The Divine Comedy of *The Tempest*." *Shakespeare Studies* 8 (1975): 279–96.

Evans, Gareth Lloyd. *The Upstart Crow: An Introduction to Shakespeare's Plays*. London: J. M. Dent, 1982.

Farnham, Willard. *The Shakespearean Grotesque: Its Genesis and Transformations.* Oxford: Clarendon, 1971.

Felperin, Howard. *Shakespearean Romance.* Princeton, N.J.: Princeton University Press, 1972.

Fergusson, Francis. *Trope and Allegory: Themes Common to Dante and Shakespeare.* Athens: University of Georgia Press, 1977.

Fiedler, Leslie A. *The Stranger in Shakespeare.* New York: Stein & Day, 1972.

Fleissner, Robert F. "The Endgame in *The Tempest.*" *Papers on Language and Literature* 21 (1985): 331–35.

Foakes, R. A. *Shakespeare: The Dark Comedies to the Last Plays: From Satire to Celebration.* London: Routledge & Kegan Paul, 1971.

Frye, Northrop. *A Natural Perspective: The Development of Shakespearean Comedy and Romance.* New York: Columbia University Press, 1965.

———. *On Shakespeare.* New Haven: Yale University Press, 1986.

———. *Spiritus Mundi: Essays on Literature, Myth, and Society.* Bloomington: Indiana University Press, 1976.

———, ed. *The Tempest.* Baltimore: Penguin, 1959.

Garber, Marjorie. *Dream in Shakespeare: From Metaphor to Metamorphosis.* New Haven: Yale University Press, 1974.

Gesner, Carol. *Shakespeare and the Greek Romance: A Study of Origins.* Lexington: University Press of Kentucky, 1970.

Gibson, William. *Shakespeare's Game.* New York: Atheneum, 1978.

Gilman, Ernest. " 'All Eyes': Prospero's Inverted Masque." *Renaissance Quarterly* 33 (1980): 214–30.

Goddard, Harold C. *The Meaning of Shakespeare.* Chicago: University of Chicago Press, 1951.

Goldman, Michael. *Shakespeare and the Energies of Drama.* Princeton, N.J.: Princeton University Press, 1972.

Gooder, R. D. "Prospero." *Cambridge Quarterly* 12 (1983): 1–25.

Grant, R. A. D. "Providence, Authority, and the Moral Life in *The Tempest.*" *Shakespeare Studies* 16 (1983): 235–63.

Harris, Anthony. *Night's Black Agents: Witchcraft and Magic in Seventeenth-Century English Drama.* Manchester, Eng.: Manchester University Press, 1980.

Hartwig, Joan. *Shakespeare's Analogical Scene: Parody as Structural Syntax.* Lincoln: University of Nebraska Press, 1983.

———. *Shakespeare's Tragicomic Vision.* Baton Rouge: Louisiana State University Press, 1972.

Hawkes, Terence. *That Shakespeherian Rag: Essays on a Critical Process.* London: Methuen, 1986.

———. *Shakespeare's Talking Animals: Language and Drama in Society.* Totowa, N.J.: Rowman & Littlefield, 1974.

Hennedy, John F. "*The Tempest* and the Counter-Renaissance." *Studies in the Humanities* 12, no. 2 (December 1985): 90–105.

Hillman, Richard. "*The Tempest* as Romance and Anti-Romance." *University of Toronto Quarterly* 55 (1985–86): 141–60.

Hirsh, James E. *The Structure of Shakespearean Scenes.* New Haven: Yale University Press, 1981.

Hobson, Alan. *Full Circle: Shakespeare and Moral Development.* London: Chatto & Windus, 1972.

Holland, Norman N. "Caliban's Dream." *Psychoanalytic Quarterly* 37 (1968): 114–25.

———. *The Shakespearean Imagination.* New York: Macmillan, 1964.

Hunter, Robert G. *Shakespeare and the Comedy of Forgiveness.* New York: Columbia University Press, 1965.

Jagendorf, Zvi. *The Happy End of Comedy: Jonson, Molière, and Shakespeare.* Newark: University of Delaware Press, 1984.

James, D. G. *The Dream of Prospero.* Oxford: Clarendon, 1967.

Johnson, W. Stacy. "The Genesis of Ariel." *Shakespeare Quarterly* 2 (1951): 205–10.

Kahn, Coppélia. "The Providential Tempest and the Shakespearean Family." In *Representing Shakespeare: New Psychoanalytic Essays,* edited by Murray M. Schwartz and Coppélia Kahn, 217–43. Baltimore: The Johns Hopkins University Press, 1980.

Kay, Carol McGinnis, and Henry E. Jacobs, eds. *Shakespeare's Romances Reconsidered.* Lincoln: University of Nebraska Press, 1978.

Kermode, Frank. *Shakespeare, Spenser, and Donne: Renaissance Essays.* London: Routledge & Kegan Paul, 1971.

———. *William Shakespeare: The Final Plays.* London: Longmans Group for British Council, 1973.

———, ed. *The Tempest.* The Arden Shakespeare. London: Methuen, 1954.

Kernan, Alvin B. *The Playwright as Magician: Shakespeare's Image of the Poet in the English Public Theater.* New Haven: Yale University Press, 1979.

Knight, G. Wilson. *The Crown of Life: Essays in Interpretation of Shakespeare's Final Plays.* London: Oxford University Press, 1947.

———. *Shakespearean Dimensions.* Totowa, N.J.: Barnes & Noble, 1984.

———. *The Shakespearean Tempest.* London: Methuen, 1960.

Knox-Shaw, Peter. " 'The Man in the Island': Shakespeare's Concern with Projection in *The Tempest.*" *Theoria* 61 (1983): 23–36.

Kott, Jan. "*The Tempest,* or Repetition." *Mosaic* 10, no. 3 (1977): 9–36.

———. *Shakespeare Our Contemporary.* Translated by Boleslaw Taborski. Garden City, N.Y.: Doubleday, 1964.

Langbaum, Robert. *The Modern Spirit.* New York: Oxford University Press, 1970.

Latham, Jacqueline E. M. "The Magic Banquet in *The Tempest.*" *Shakespeare Studies* 12 (1979): 215–27.

———. "*The Tempest* and King James's *Daemonology.*" *Shakespeare Studies* 8 (1975): 117–24.

Leech, Clifford. *Shakespeare's Tragedies and Other Studies in Seventeeth Century Drama.* 1950. Reprint. Westport, Conn.: Greenwood, 1975.

Leininger, Lorie Jerrell. "The Miranda Trap: Sexism and Racism in Shakespeare's *Tempest.*" In *The Woman's Part: Feminist Criticism of Shakespeare,* edited by Carolyn Ruth Swift Lenz, et al., 285–94. Urbana: University of Illinois Press, 1980.

Lindenbaum, Peter. "Prospero's Anger." *Massachusetts Review* 25 (1984): 161–71.

McFarland, Thomas. *Shakespeare's Pastoral Comedy.* Chapel Hill: University of North Carolina Press, 1972.

McGuire, Philip C. *Speechless Dialect: Shakespeare's Open Silences.* Berkeley: University of California Press, 1985.

Manlove, Colin N. *The Gap in Shakespeare: The Motif of Division from* Richard II *to* The Tempest. London: Vision, 1981.

Muir, Kenneth. *Last Periods of Shakespeare, Racine, and Ibsen.* Detroit: Wayne State University Press, 1961.

———. *Shakespeare's Comic Sequence.* New York: Barnes & Noble, 1979.

Murry, John Middleton. *Shakespeare.* London: Jonathan Cape, 1936.

Neill, Michael. "Remembrance and Revenge: *Hamlet, Macbeth,* and *The Tempest.*" In *Jonson and Shakespeare,* edited by Ian Donaldson. London: Macmillan, 1983.

Novy, Marianne. *Love's Argument: Gender Relations in Shakespeare.* Chapel Hill: University of North Carolina Press, 1984.

Nuttall, A. D. "Two Unassimilable Men." In *Shakespearean Comedy.* London: E. Arnold, 1972.

———. *Two Concepts of Allegory: A Study of Shakespeare's* The Tempest *and the Logic of Allegorical Expression.* London: Routledge & Kegan Paul, 1967.

Orgel, Stephen. "New Uses of Adversity: Tragic Experience in *The Tempest.*" In *In Defense of Reading,* edited by Reuben Brower and Richard Poirier. New York: Dutton, 1962.

———. "Shakespeare and the Cannibals." In *Cannibals, Witches, and Divorce: Estranging the Renaissance,* edited by Marjorie Garber, 40–66. Baltimore: The Johns Hopkins University Press, 1987.

Ornstein, Robert. *Shakespeare's Comedies: From Roman Farce to Romantic Mystery.* Newark: University of Delaware Press, 1986.

Palmer, D. J. *Shakespeare's Later Comedies.* Baltimore: Penguin, 1971.

Pearson, D'Orsay W. " 'Unless I Be Relieved by Prayer': *The Tempest* in Perspective." *Shakespeare Studies* 7 (1974): 253–82.

Peterson, Douglas L. *Time, Tide, and Tempest: A Study of Shakespeare's Romances.* San Marino, Calif.: Huntington Library, 1973.

Pierce, Robert B. " 'Very Like a Whale': Skepticism and Seeing in *The Tempest.*" *Shakespeare Survey* 38 (1985): 167–74.

Potter, A. M. "Possession, Surrender, and Freedom in *The Tempest.*" *Theoria* 61 (1983): 37–49.

Rabkin, Norman. *Shakespeare and the Common Understanding.* New York: Free Press, 1967.

———, ed. *Approaches to Shakespeare.* New York: McGraw-Hill, 1964.

Riemer, A. P. *Antic Fables: Patterns of Evasion in Shakespeare's Comedies.* New York: St. Martin's, 1980.

Righter, Anne [Anne Barton]. *Shakespeare and the Idea of the Play.* Westport, Conn.: Greenwood, 1962.

———, ed. *The Tempest.* The Penguin Shakespeare. Baltimore: Penguin, 1968.

Roberts, Jeanne Addison. " 'Wife' or 'Wise'—*The Tempest* l. 1786." *University of Virginia Studies in Bibliography* 31 (1978): 203–8.

Schmidgall, Gary. *Shakespeare and the Courtly Aesthetic.* Berkeley: University of California Press, 1981.

Shanker, Sidney. *Shakespeare and the Uses of Ideology.* The Hague: Mouton, 1975.

Sharp, Sister Corona. "Caliban: The Primitive Man's Evolution." *Shakespeare Studies* 14 (1981): 267–83.

Sisson, C. J. "The Magic of Prospero." *Shakespeare Survey* 11 (1958): 70–77.

Slover, George. "Magic, Mystery, and Make-Believe: An Analogical Reading of *The Tempest*." *Shakespeare Studies* 11 (1978): 175–206.

Smith, Hallet. *Shakespeare's Romances: A Study of Some Ways of the Imagination*. San Marino, Calif.: Huntington Library, 1972.

———, ed. *Twentieth-Century Interpretations of* The Tempest: *A Collection of Critical Essays*. Englewood Cliffs, N.J.: Prentice-Hall, 1969.

Srigley, Michael. *Images of Regeneration: A Study of Shakespeare's* The Tempest *and Its Cultural Background*. Uppsala, Sweden: Almqvist & Wiksell, 1985.

Stoll, E. E. *Shakespeare and Other Masters*. New York: Russell & Russell, 1962.

Summers, Joseph. *Dreams of Love and Power: On Shakespeare's Plays*. Oxford: Clarendon, 1984.

Sundelson, David. *Shakespeare's Restorations of the Father*. New Brunswick, N.J.: Rutgers University Press, 1983.

Tillyard, E. M. W. *Shakespeare's Last Plays*. London: Chatto & Windus, 1938.

Traversi, Derek. *An Approach to Shakespeare*. London: Hollis & Carter, 1969.

———. *Shakespeare: The Last Phase*. Stanford: Stanford University Press, 1965.

Van Laan, Thomas F. *Role-Playing in Shakespeare*. Toronto: University of Toronto Press, 1978.

Velie, Alan R. *Shakespeare's Repentance Plays: The Search for an Adequate Form*. Rutherford, N.J.: Fairleigh Dickinson University Press, 1972.

Welsford, Enid. *The Court Masque: A Study in the Relationship between Poetry and the Revels*. 1927. Reprint. New York: Russell & Russell, 1962.

West, Robert H. *Shakespeare and the Outer Mystery*. Lexington: University Press of Kentucky, 1968.

Wickham, Glynne. "Masque and Anti-masque in *The Tempest*." *Essays and Studies* 28 (1975): 1–14.

William, David. "*The Tempest* on the Stage." In *Jacobean Theatre*, edited by John Russell Brown and Bernard Harris, 133–57. Stratford-Upon-Avon Studies, no. 1. London: E. Arnold, 1960.

Yates, Frances A. *Shakespeare's Last Plays: A New Approach*. London: Routledge & Kegan Paul, 1975.

Yoch, James J., Jr. "Subjecting the Landscape in Pageants and Shakespearean Pastorals." In *Pageantry in the Shakespearean Theater*, edited by David Bergeron, 194–219. Athens: University of Georgia Press, 1985.

Young, David. *The Heart's Forest: A Study of Shakespeare's Pastoral Plays*. New Haven: Yale University Press, 1972.

Acknowledgments

"Miraculous Harp: A Reading of Shakespeare's *Tempest*" by Harry Berger, Jr., from *Shakespeare Studies* 5 (1969), © 1970 by the Center for Shakespeare Studies. Reprinted by permission.

"The Eye of the Storm: Structure and Myth in Shakespeare's *Tempest*" by Marjorie Garber from *The Hebrew University Studies in Literature* 8, no. 1 (Spring 1980), © 1980 by HSL, The Hebrew University, Jerusalem. Reprinted by permission of the editors.

"Learning to Curse: Linguistic Colonialism in *The Tempest*" (originally entitled "Learning to Curse: Aspects of Linguistic Colonialism in the Sixteenth Century") by Stephen J. Greenblatt from *First Images of America: The Impact of the New World on the Old,* vol. 2, edited by Fredi Chiappelli, © 1976 by the Regents of the University of California. Reprinted by permission of the University of California Press.

"*The Tempest* as Supplement" by Julian Patrick from *Centre and Labyrinth: Essays in Honour of Northrop Frye,* edited by Eleanor Cook, Chaviva Hosek, Jay Macpherson, Patricia Parker, and Julian Patrick, © 1983 by the University of Toronto Press. Reprinted by permission of the University of Toronto Press.

"The Shakespearean 'Metastance' " by James P. Driscoll from *Identity in Shakespearean Drama* by James P. Driscoll, © 1983 by Associated University Presses, Inc. Reprinted by permission of Associated University Presses, Inc.

"Prospero's Wife" by Stephen Orgel from *Representations* 8 (Fall 1984), © 1984 by the Regents of the University of California. Reprinted by permission of the Regents.

"Prospero: Master of Self-knowledge" by Barbara Howard Traister from *Heavenly Necromancers: The Magician in English Renaissance Drama* by Barbara Howard Traister, © 1984 by the Curators of the University of Missouri. Reprinted by permission of the University of Missouri Press.

" 'This Thing of Darkness I Acknowledge Mine': *The Tempest* and the Discourse of Colonialism" by Paul Brown from *Political Shakespeare: New Essays in Cultural Materialism,* edited by Jonathan Dollimore and Alan Sinfield, © 1985 by Paul Brown. Reprinted by permission of Manchester University Press.

Index